C0-AYG-637

THE JESUS OF PSYCHOANALYSIS

A Freudian Interpretation
of the Gospel

A Freudian Interpretation
of the Gospel

The Jesus of
Psychoanalysis

Françoise Dolto and Gérard Séverin

Translated by Helen R. Lane

DOUBLEDAY & COMPANY, INC.
GARDEN CITY, NEW YORK

1979

0261969
54513

This book was originally published in French under the title
L'Évangile au risque de la psychanalyse, © Jean-Pierre Delarge,
Éditions universitaires, 1977.
Excerpts from the Jerusalem Bible, copyright © 1966 by Darton,
Longman & Todd Ltd. and Doubleday & Company, Inc. Used by
permission of the publisher.

Library of Congress Cataloging in Publication Data

Dolto, Françoise Marette.
   The Jesus of psychoanalysis.

   1. Jesus Christ—Psychology. I. Sévérin, Gérard,
joint author. II. Title.
BT590.P9D6413   232.9′001′9
ISBN: 0-385-14542-X
Library of Congress Catalog Card Number: 78-60287

English Translation Copyright © 1979 by Doubleday &
Company, Inc.
All Rights Reserved
Printed in the United States of America
First Edition

CONTENTS

	INTRODUCTION	11
Chapter I	THE "HOLY FAMILY"	21
Chapter II	IN THE TEMPLE	35
Chapter III	LIKE A LITTLE CHILD	43
Chapter IV	CANA	53
Chapter V	AT THE FOOT OF THE CROSS	63
Chapter VI	RESURRECTIONS FROM THE DEAD	71
	Foreword	73
	The Raising of the Son of the Widow of Nain	77
	The Healing of the Woman with a Hemorrhage and the Raising of the Daughter of Jairus	103
	The Raising of Lazarus	121
Chapter VII	THE OINTMENT OF BETHANY	135
Chapter VIII	THE PARABLE OF THE SAMARITAN	145

0261969
54512

AUTHORS' NOTE

For reasons of convenience and in order to render the text of this work more vivid, we have used the imperfect [past continuous] tense. This might lead our readers to think that we are taking a position with regard to the historicity of Gospel texts. In this book we wish to take no part in such controversies.

We merely bear witness to the fact that the most profound questions raised by psychoanalysis in its dynamic effects have found their echo in us. It seems to us that these same questions had already seen the light of day in the texts of the Gospels.

They constitute a story in the present, still vividly alive: we are the same humanity.

TRANSLATOR'S NOTE

For the biblical texts cited, I have followed the Jerusalem Bible. Where Gérard Sévérin's and Françoise Dolto's comments are closer to the King James Version, I have cited this version in footnotes.

HRL

THE JESUS OF
PSYCHOANALYSIS

INTRODUCTION

Gérard Séverin

*It is rare to find psychoanalysts who describe them-
selves in public as believers and Christians.*

*It is rare to find a psychoanalyst who agrees to express
and explain her faith in the Gospels.*

*It is really very rarely that a psychoanalyst does not re-
fuse to allow the fruit of years of spiritual life and human
clinical experience to be made into a book and put before
others.*

*Why have you consented to reveal your way of rejoic-
ing or of enjoying your encounter with the Gospels of Jesus
Christ?*

Françoise Dolto

In my childhood I heard the texts of the Gospels at
church—or read them—as though they were passages from a
story, that of Jesus and the world of his time and the sun-
drenched places in which he lived.

That story happened "in the old days," as elderly people in my family said when they talked of their childhood,
but the story went even farther back than that. That set me
to dreaming, and then illustrations, paintings proved to me
that this story set everyone to dreaming, and I discovered
that everyone had his own way of dreaming about it. But I
for my part could see no link between these stories and my
own life and that of the people around me—those of the
Church hierarchy, or the "faithful," as they were called.

And then I grew up, as people still say today; I
suffered, I was psychoanalyzed, I became a doctor and a
psychoanalyst. The sacred texts of our Greco-Judeo-Chris-

tian civilization came to seem more and more important to me.

The Bible, the Gospels, began to ask me questions and I began to react to my reading of them. I was surprised that my interest in them was continually renewed as I experienced life and especially as I engaged in clinical psychoanalytic practice, in the discovery of the dynamics of the unconscious as, since Freud, we have come to understand it, its strength and the decoding of its laws.

It seems to me these texts reveal what we discover about human beings. The unconscious speaks in this treasure of collected works.

But how did you come to have the idea of presenting your reflections on these texts to readers?

On meeting Jean-Pierre Delarge, the publisher, at a dinner one night, the conversation happened to turn to the parable of the Good Samaritan and its illustration of the concept of "one's neighbor" by means of which Jesus teaches us whom to love. I said that it was not a question of a moral lesson; it was not a question of acts voluntarily and consciously engaged in but of a school of unconscious desire that we should allow to come to us; not a school wherein we should force desire to constrain itself and then enjoy our charitable act as though it were a conquest, then later attempt to repeat charitable acts falsely—any more than it was a question of criticizing those who lacked charity in our eyes.

This way of reading the Gospels that I spoke of as my personal experience seemed new to those who were present and made me feel like a "barbarian" in the midst of these well-educated Christians; I admired the text of the parable for reasons completely different from theirs.

The text of this parable did not seem to me to be at all in accord with the so-called Christian moral lesson that had been drawn from it. It seemed to me to reveal, rather, an unconscious dynamic centered on solidarity between human beings who fail to recognize each other, who do not know each other, as well as a cohesive inner dynamic revealed to each one of us.

It seemed to me that this lesson revealed to us an almost sacred connection between love and freedom insofar as the relations between individuals are concerned and between the feeling of freedom and the feeling of love insofar as the psychic structure of the desiring subject in each one of us is concerned.

Jean-Pierre Delarge said to me that evening: "You must write that." I tried to do so. For years I would write and then cross out what I had written. It appeared to me to be a difficult, if not impossible, task all by myself. It was at this point, Gérard Séverin, that I spoke to you of this project, one evening when we were having dinner at your place. You were interested and offered to help me—you, of course, were also a psychoanalyst and you, out of your own desire, were passionately interested in this research. And your wife has also helped the two of us in this task by transcribing our tape-recorded conversation.

Yes, but you were a psychoanalyst before I was. How long before you had that meeting with our publisher did you begin this study, and why?

Why? I really don't know why except for the fact that as regards human psychology, Freud's discoveries seemed as revolutionary as the Copernican revolution.

The Church in its time could not accept the discoveries of Copernicus, nor later those of Galileo. And yet what was there that was contradictory in the message of the Bible?

For me it was the same adventure as with the discovery of the role of the unconscious in the structure of our psychic life and the structuring processes of the human being that psychoanalysis has revealed to us. The Church and its faithful "resisted" Freud's discoveries. Pansexuality! That was unthinkable—an abomination! And yet I knew from experience that Freud and the research that had been done after him, using his method, proved each day the existence of this unconscious, of this desire at work in the human being—unmasked truth—which was truer than the behavior of those moral, disciplined, sad, and intractable beings in their so-called virtuous behavior, deprived as they were of spontaneity, joy, and respect for that nature that lives in man.

I discovered this so-called Christian education received by so many of our patients to be the enemy of life and charity, in total contradiction with what had seemed to me to be at one time the message of joy and love in the Gospels. So I reread them then—and was shocked.

Nothing of what the Church of the twentieth century taught to those who were brought up in it seemed to me to be contained either in the Bible as a whole or in the Gospels and nothing in Christ's message contradicted Freudian discoveries. There and then I decided to continue my reading.

And what did this reading bring you?

What did it bring me? That's the wrong tense: it is still bringing me things!

As one who has had psychoanalytic training, what I read in the Gospels seems to me to be the confirmation, the illustration of that living dynamic at work in the human life of the psyche and its force which comes from the unconscious, where desire has its source, where it departs on the search for what it is lacking.

Life, the effect of ever-new truth that familiarity with the Gospels brings to the human heart and intelligence, is a summons renewed from day to day, to go beyond our conscious logical processes. They remain the same words and yet they seem to reveal a new meaning as we live out our days, as our experience unfolds. That is what passionately interests me.

The Gospels continually question us, no matter what answers we have already found. How do these texts, these series of words, come to shock our consciousness and send shock waves into our unconscious, bringing to life resources of joy and the desire to know, to know this kingdom of God?

So you can see why I dare to publish my reflections. And there are certainly a good many reasons—as I call them; reasons that the existence of each of us participates in, as the Gospels reveal to us—that I know nothing of and that certainly are narcissistic—why wouldn't they be?

To read the Gospels is to understand about those who saw, understood, and bore witness to that being of flesh and blood, Jesus, when he lived on earth in his individuality that is no longer there for our eyes to see. He speaks to my presently individual being. He speaks to my heart and summons my intelligence to listen to him and to desire to meet him. And you, do you not desire, as I do, to go there where he is, there where we are seeking him, since he has invited all of us—children, barbarians, the down-and-out, the educated, all of us—by his words and his acts, milestones along the path that is there to follow till the end of time?

Are we not also, we who are psychoanalysts by training and profession, able to speak of him by questioning each other, as others have done, as others are doing and will do, in another way—all of us summoned, through desire, to seek him?

The criticism that might be leveled against you is that using a word, a phrase, from the Gospels as your point of departure, you say a great many things—on castration, for example, or on the life of desire, and so on. In other words, on reading your work, will the reader not find more Françoise Dolto than Jesus himself, your theory or your unconscious rather than the Gospels?

On reading the Gospels, I find a psychodrama. The very words that they use to tell their story—the choice of phrases, the selection of certain themes—can be understood, I repeat, in a different way since Freud's discovery of the unconscious and its laws. Today's discoveries in psychoanalysis—a dialectic and a dynamic of the unconscious, as I read them—are illustrated by this psychodrama that is related to us.

The laws of Jesus' unconscious, of the Gospel writers, and of the first hearers are the principal factors in the elaboration of the Gospels. These laws constitute an integral part of the structure of these stories. Why not approach the reading of them with this new tool, psychoanalysis?

But then do you psychoanalyze Jesus, Mark, Matthew, John, and so on?

Not at all. The reading of the Gospels, I repeat, produces first of all a shock to my subjectivity, and then, on further contact with these texts, I discover that Jesus teaches desire and guides us to desire.

I discover that these two thousand-year-old texts are not contradictory to the unconscious of men of today.

I discover that these texts illustrate and shed light on the laws of the unconscious discovered in the last century. That is all.

Hence these texts have the same power as fairy tales?

They have a power that is even more surprising. They have been read for two thousand years, as I have said, and they still have the ring of truth in the heart of hearts of every person who reads them. I am interested in tracing the sources of this truth.

Whether they are historical facts or not, these texts are a fantastic torrent of the sublimation of impulses. Writings that are this striking cannot be neglected. They deserve from us who are trained in psychoanalysis, that we search for the key of this dynamic that they have suggested.

Chapter I

THE "HOLY FAMILY"

54910

54513

The Gospel According to Saint Luke
Chapter I, Verses 26 to 38

26 In the sixth month the angel Gabriel was sent by God to a
27 town in Galilee called Nazareth, ·to a virgin betrothed to a
man named Joseph, of the House of David; and the virgin's
28 name was Mary. ·He went in and said to her, "Rejoice, so
29 highly favored! The Lord is with you." ·She was deeply disturbed by these words and asked herself what this greeting
30 could mean, ·but the angel said to her, "Mary, do not be
31 afraid; you have won God's favor. ·Listen! You are to con-
32 ceive and bear a son, and you must name him Jesus. ·He will
be great and will be called Son of the Most High. The Lord
33 God will give him the throne of his ancestor David; ·he will
rule over the House of Jacob for ever and his reign will have
34 no end." ·Mary said to the angel, "But how can this come
35 about, since I am a virgin?" ·"The Holy Spirit will come upon
you," the angel answered, "and the power of the Most High
will cover you with its shadow. And so the child will be holy
36 and will be called Son of God. ·Know this too: your kins-
woman Elizabeth has, in her old age, herself conceived a son,
and she whom people called barren is now in her sixth month,
37
38 for nothing is impossible to God." ·"I am the handmaid of
the Lord," said Mary, "let what you have said be done to me."
And the angel left her.

The Gospel According to Saint Matthew
Chapter I, Verses 18 to 25

18 This is how Jesus Christ came to be born. His mother Mary
was betrothed to Joseph; but before they came to live together
19 she was found to be with child through the Holy Spirit. ·Her
husband Joseph, being a man of honor and wanting to spare
20 her publicity, decided to divorce her informally. ·He had made
up his mind to do this when the angel of the Lord appeared

to him in a dream and said, "Joseph son of David, do not be afraid to take Mary home as your wife, because she has con-
21 ceived what is in her by the Holy Spirit. ·She will give birth to a son and you must name him Jesus, because he is the one
22 who is to save his people from their sins." ·Now all this took place to fulfill the words spoken by the Lord through the prophet:

23   The virgin will conceive and give birth to a son
        and they will call him Immanuel,

24 a name which means "God-is-with-us." ·When Joseph woke up he did what the angel of the Lord had told him to do: he
25 took his wife to his home ·and, though he had not had intercourse with her, she gave birth to a son; and he named him Jesus.

Gérard Séverin

Joseph is a man without a woman. Mary is a woman without a man. Jesus is a child without a father. Can we speak, then, of a real family?

Françoise Dolto

Yes, we can speak of a real family, in terms of responsibility before the law.

The animal family does not exist before the law. The "family" is a human term which involves the mutual responsibility of the parents for the raising of a child before the law.

The family is also the source of the participation in goods, in the common fortune of the group, as well as in its common trials, along with a way of living and of speaking that is in accordance with the customs of the group.

But your question comes from the fact that in this part of the Gospels, there is a certain amount of myth.

Well, then, what does a myth signify to you?

It is a projection of preverbal imaginary constructs, of the feeling of living in one's body. When I say "mythical," I mean beyond the particular imaginary constructs of each one of us; it is a meeting of all imaginary constructs superimposed in one and the same representation.

One could say more precisely that a myth always tells us how something is born. We witness here the birth of Jesus Christ and of the New Testament.

Myth also is part of a mystery—that is to say, it reveals a truth. This myth of the origins of Christianity is rich and full of meaning.

Very often one accepts the grandeur and the human richness of Greek or Hindu mythologies, for instance, whereas on this same plane, the resources of Judeo-Christian myths are neglected. It is true that these traditions concern the believer on another plane. Might there be a certain fear of the beyond and of the transcendent that prevents the majority of unbelievers from sharing in them?

I have no doubt of that. I for my part am convinced that the "Holy Family," as Catholics say, or the Gospels which recount the childhood of Jesus are expressed by mythical images but they also convey a mystery, a truth, that is revealed in their texts.

There is myth in these passages of the Gospel. That is beyond question. But for me, as a believer and a psychoanalyst, that is not all there is.

With all our biological, scientific knowledge, what do we know of love and its mystery? What do we know of joy?

And likewise, what do we know of the spoken word? Is it not something that grows? Is it not sometimes the bearer of death?

What do we know of that extraordinary alchemy represented by grafts in the vegetable kingdom, a phenomenon that is nonetheless natural? Even Vergil long ago celebrated this miracle! He speaks of the grafted vine that is astonished to bear fruits upon its branches that it does not even recognize!

And what if the word Mary received was God's graft on this branch of David?

And even if this is not so, I see nothing basically objectionable in the fact that Jesus, as a man, was conceived as a result of the carnal union of Mary and Joseph! In point of fact, this carnal union is not what is responsible for making the fate of Jesus as a man the total incarnation of God.

You can understand, then, why all the gynecological discussions about the Virgin strike me as imbecilic quibbles, as do the mocking innuendos about Joseph's marital status.

The angel announced to Mary: "The power of God will cover you with its shadow." Where is Joseph in that?

For a woman who loves her man, is not every man the shadow of God?

The power and the shadow that God has over Mary may be the carnality of a man that she recognizes as her spouse.

And yet it seems that Joseph does not recognize himself as Mary's spouse or at least not as the begetter of Jesus. In fact, he wishes to repudiate Mary when he learns that she is with child. And elsewhere Mary says: "I do not know man."

We must seek to discover what these texts mean.

This revelation of the conception of Jesus is made to Mary in her waking state and to Joseph in his sleep, in a dream. That is to say that the phallic powers, the feminine creators of Mary's desire are awakened, in a state of readiness and openness, whereas the passive powers of Joseph's desire are at their maximum.

In other words, Mary desires. Through the intervention of the angel (and this is a mythical way of speaking), she knows that she will be with child. But how? She has no idea. But like every woman, she hopes, she desires to be pregnant with an exceptional being.

As for Joseph, he knows, through the instruction received in his sleep, that in order to bring a son of God into the world, it is necessary for the man to believe that he has had very little to do with this.

We are far, as you can see, from all the stories of parturition and coitus. What is described here is a mode of relation to the symbolic phallus, that is to say, to the fundamental lack of every being. These Gospels describe how the other, in a couple, never entirely fulfills his partner, how there is always a gap, a lack, an impossible encounter and not a relationship, with possession, with phallocracy, with dependence.

There is nothing about Joseph that is possessive of his woman. Just as in Mary there is nothing that is *a priori* possessive of her child. As an engaged couple, they trust life, and their destiny as a couple follows from this. They accept this.

One would almost think that they were a couple of today, an unmarried couple!

On the contrary, they are an exemplary married couple: their child is not the fruit of passion but of love.

Their desire is described as transcended in the love of their family line, and what is more, they have given their life, their destiny over to the fulfillment of Scripture.

For me it is because they are obedient to Scripture, that is to say, to the written Word of God that they are an exemplary couple, a couple who cleave to the Word as given, the Word as received.

The Word that is given has come from the creative and fecundating Word as received. The Word given to be the guarantor of this woman, the Word given to make this child their own. The Word given to be trustful, to be a mother without knowing how . . .

The Word heard by Joseph, who sees that his wife is with child when he does not feel himself to be the one responsible for this pregnancy. He is told in his sleep: "She is bearing the child of God, do not abandon her."

The Word listened to in order to save the child, on the eve of the slaughter of the innocents, again in his sleep, in a dream! And Joseph bows to this demand for obedience asked of him when this child is perhaps not the child of his flesh.

And so he was perhaps not the father?

Perhaps not! But it must be pointed out that often there is a confusion between father and begetter. It takes a man a moment in time to become a begetter. To be a father is another adventure altogether.

To be a father is to give one's name to a child, to pay for the subsistence of this child by the sweat of one's brow, to bring him up, to educate him; it means to call him to more life, more desire . . . That is quite a different thing from being a begetter. So much the better, perhaps, if the father is the begetter, but, you know, there are only adoptive fathers.

A father must always "adopt" his child. There are those who adopt their child at his birth, others a few days later, even several weeks later; others will adopt him when he begins to talk; and so on. There are only adoptive fathers.

And I shall add that a man is never sure of being the procreator; he must trust the word of his wife.

And so the complexity of the human relationship of each couple can be found in the story of the couple formed by Joseph and Mary. But on the other hand this extraordinary couple helps us to discover what a profound experience the encounter between an ordinary man and an ordinary woman can be.

But what would it be like to be a family today in which the mother was a virgin—or a virgin a mother?

That is what we come across every day. Every son would like his mother to be a virgin. This is a fantasy that looms up out of the night of time, while the son was in his mother's womb. He had no rival there. He knows of the existence of his mother's man only when he can hear, see, and discriminate the forms of those surrounding his mother. Hence, during a very long period of his life, through his imaginary heterosexual desires that anticipate his life as an adult, a boy can believe that he fulfills his mother's desire. As an adolescent he would like to continue his life in accordance with the primordial circumstances of his desire.

But the virginity that the Gospels speak of is after all something quite different from badly liquidated fantasies!

0261962

Yes, of course . . . To be a virgin is to be open. For the woman who is a virgin, for the man who is a virgin, the Word becomes more important than the flesh. Here the Word of God is more important than the flesh.

It is for that reason, it seems to me, that the Church wishes Mary to be a virgin before and after her lying-in, as though she had given birth to a Word, as though it were a Word, the Word of God, a Word that had come forth from her and not a carnal mass that had sprung forth, in space, by way of her carnal body as a procreator.

In every human being, whether it is a man or a woman, are a man and a woman, and therefore both Joseph and Mary, the lover who gives and the lover who receives.

We all have a tendency toward maternity that may be virgin and remain virgin, and likewise a tendency toward paternity. What does this mean? It simply means that we can bear the fruits of a Word received from another.

Our thought may grow from an idea that has come from elsewhere, without our knowing who has given it to us. Isn't what is psychologically true capable of being spiritually true?

That is what Mary represents: she is an image, a metaphor of perfect openness. That is what Joseph represents; his virginity, his chastity as a husband and father mediate the same truth: being open. Both of them, she in the waking state, he fast asleep, welcome the Word of God. The desire in their flesh acquiesces to that of God who desires to incarnate himself as a man.

The important thing is that words relating the incarnation of God in human terms continue to raise a problem: they continually raise the question of our relationship to desire and love.

The fantasy of the virgin-mother, a male fantasy, finds its echo here. By identifying first with Jesus and then with John the Evangelist, in a love of Mary that goes from heart to heart, a man redeems and transcends his fetal, oral, carnal attachment as an individual that is carried, borne, and nourished by his human mother. Why not? Mary serves then as a transfer and a relay for all filial love.

And girls, wives, or mothers can also identify strongly with Mary, with their hearts that are so often wounded, both by their own mother and by male lack of understanding.

For you, Mary and Joseph are beings of flesh and blood and representative figures—I was about to say models.

Mary is precisely that, the womanly representative of total receptivity to God, in a state of wakefulness.

Joseph is the representation of the total receptivity to the Word of God, in a state of sleep.

The active sleeps: the man is active in his creative, genital emission.

The passive is awake and listening: the woman is passive in her genital receptivity.

This is perhaps an example to reflect upon, concerning the conscious and unconscious openness which does not speak, which listens to God.

Joseph is an extraordinary example, for he agrees in his very unconscious to raise this child. He knows that one never has the children that one dreams of, and he adopts him. He agrees to protect him, to guide him, to instruct him in the law, to teach him his craft as a man, without being his rival.

Don't the words that recount this have an exemplary value for us who censure our children instead of accepting them and who behave like octopuses toward our children out of fear or a sense of rivalry?

Let's review what we've discussed. We could say that for you all questions concerning the virginity of Mary, the marital status of Joseph, and so on, are, in the end, questions that are not of very great importance.

As a matter of fact, for me they are false questions because everything concerning our spiritual life is an offense to the flesh. Everything that resembles logic to the flesh makes no sense from the moment that we are questioned by our spiritual life, when we are desirous of a spiritual life.

We know, of course, as psychoanalysts, that carnal life can be a trap for desire, but just because that may be true does not mean that it is always true.

We likewise know that spiritual life—but is this only a spiritual life?—we know that spiritual life can be a sort of supernarcissism: we begin to love, for example, our own words that we say to God, our words, our phonemes, that we beam toward God! But the fact that prayer risks being this does not mean that that is always what it is!

Prayer is beyond all our phonemes, beyond all sounds. It resides in a silence, in a muteness that is unknown to humans among themselves. A muteness sounding the clarion of desire whose force every man, every woman, feels at some moment in his or her life, summoning him or her to live a spiritual life. This desire can make one fearless.

I can no longer see the relation that you feel exists between this spiritual life, this offense to the flesh, and the "Holy Family."

But the "Holy Family"—which might not be considered a family since it appears not to be ordinary in the genital sense, on the human plane—this family serves as a focus of all the genital needs on the spiritual plane. It shows how one is born to, how one responds to, spiritual life.

You see a man who believes in the power of words, though he is in a deep sleep. That is not logical! A man believes in acts, in the power of his body, in the power of his sex in which he invests his pride, as a witness of himself.

You see a woman, totally powerless, who, in the waking state, believes in the possibility that God is made manifest through her!

All this is completely against logic, surrealistic—and yet Mary and Joseph live a full, everyday life. They leave for Egypt in order that Jesus may escape being massacred at the hands of Herod's soldiers. They are not rich. They are little people who have the intelligence of the flesh, of the heart, and of the spiritual life.

Chapter II

IN
THE
TEMPLE

The Gospel According to Saint Luke
Chapter II, Verses 42 to 52

⁴² When he was twelve years old, they went up for the feast as
⁴³ usual. ·When they were on their way home after the feast,
the boy Jesus stayed behind in Jerusalem without his parents
⁴⁴ knowing it. ·They assumed he was with the caravan, and it
was only after a day's journey that they went to look for him
⁴⁵ among their relations and acquaintances. ·When they failed
to find him they went back to Jerusalem looking for him
everywhere.
⁴⁶　　Three days later, they found him in the Temple, sitting
among the doctors, listening to them, and asking them ques-
⁴⁷ tions; ·and all those who heard him were astounded at his
⁴⁸ intelligence and his replies. ·They were overcome when they
saw him, and his mother said to him, "My child, why have
you done this to us? See how worried your father and I have
⁴⁹ been, looking for you." ·"Why were you looking for me?" he
replied. "Did you not know that I must be busy with my Fa-
⁵⁰ ther's affairs?" ·But they did not understand what he meant.
⁵¹　　He then went down with them and came to Nazareth and
lived under their authority. His mother stored up all these
⁵² things in her heart. ·And Jesus increased in wisdom, in stature, and in favor with God and men.

Gérard Sévérin

*Could Jesus have lived through that fundamental com-
plex that is known as the "Oedipus complex"? More simply
stated, was Jesus castrated, separated from his mother by
Joseph?*

Françoise Dolto

Normally, the boy resolves this separation from his

mother around the age of five or six. I believe that Jesus must have lived through this castration at that age, judging by this episode in the Temple. If he had not resolved his Oedipus complex, he could not have experienced this turn of events in this way.

What happened that was so extraordinary?

Jesus enters adult life. Thus it is he who castrates his parents of their possessiveness.

How could Joseph and Mary have become possessive toward their child?

The permanent presence of Jesus in their home allows them, like all parents, to believe that this child is theirs, that he belongs to them.

Moreover, doesn't Mary herself say: "My child, why have you done this to us?" As though she thought that Jesus had intentionally played a naughty trick on them! If Jesus acts as he sees fit or if he acts according to the vocation that he believes is his, his parents are affected by it.

For Mary, what Jesus lives is directed against herself and Joseph: "He is doing this to us!" You can see that the life of the parents and that of the child are deeply involved with each other here, closely linked. Is this not what it means to be possessive toward a child, like all parents in the world, if they are not careful?

And so, as each child must do, Jesus, I repeat, castrates his parents of their possessiveness. He thereby demonstrates to us the exemplary development of a child in a family.

He is twelve or thirteen years old; he is on the threshold of adult life.

He does not abandon his parents, but he is no longer their child. He is their son.

Among the Jews, a boy is a man at the age of twelve or thirteen. Thus a synagogue is not first and foremost a stone building but, rather, a place where there are ten men who are thirteen years of age and older. They represent the community. The synagogue is a *place*, in the human and social meaning of the term.

Hence Jesus says to his parents: "I must be busy with my Father's affairs." They know this, but they are not aware that Jesus already knows this too. They do not understand. They are very anxious and this separation hurts them. But all this has penetrated their hearts, which continue to bear its traces.

Jesus now accepts, therefore, the knowledge that he is God's, that he must be about his Father's business. He has "killed" the child Jesus! A "sword of pain" pierces the hearts of his parents. But in what respect is he exemplary?

First of all, Jesus separates himself from Mary as a human mother: "I do not belong to you, I was your child but now I am busy with my Father's business. I have my own way to follow, my vocation."

And then for Joseph, Jesus plays the role of revealer. He repeats the explanation of the Angel to Joseph in his sleep: "You were not deceived, I do not belong to you, I am that child of the Almighty."

He belongs neither to Mary nor to Joseph.

He nonetheless bows to the authority of Joseph in order to go on with his adolescence. He recognizes in this father the one who has given him human arms and who has trained him, for it is necessary to be physically strong in order to become a carpenter. It is going to be necessary for him to be physically strong in order to drive the money changers from the Temple. Jesus does not grow up as an intellectual who lives only in books or as a backward young man, apparently submissive, out of fear or dependence, with a perpetual account to settle with his father.

It is proper for a boy to separate from his mother and discover the direction to be taken in his life with the aid and support of his father.

Jesus' childhood ends with this significant event. The man in Jesus blossoms forth. Through words that are incomprehensible to his parents, he says that he accepts the desire to which his family line calls him.

Hence Jesus cuts his parents off from himself, as all parents should be from their child. In this respect, he is an example to follow. But what about this scene where he has a "starring role" as a child prodigy?

After disappearing, Jesus is found again by his anxious parents: he now feels responsible for his Father's affairs. The matter is settled—the spiritual education of Jesus has come to an end. He is twelve years old; he knows, he affirms, he declares his vocation.

It is a vocation in the sense that he feels called, attracted, and his desire to answer this summons arouses in him forces that enable him to let go of the past and orient both his life and all his desire toward answering this summons.

He must thus have been aware of a summons and have had both the strength and the desire to answer it.

He feels magnetized by an aspiration. In order to arrive at this point, he leaves behind all other, parasitical desires. Attracted by the invitation that he is aware of, he cannot help but answer it; otherwise he would deny his own self. It is a matter of secondary importance, then, that he feels anguish at distressing his parents, who had not counted on their child's taking this direction, who did not expect him to become so different from them so fast.

Many children, from the age of twelve onward, feel the desire to embrace a way of life; they dream of it, they prepare themselves for it.

Yes, and this outgoing impulse, this desire is always to be respected, even if the parents are able to understand nothing at all about this legitimate but infrequent desire.

Many children are led astray, however, by a desire that lasts a long time and does not die away.

That is also true. That is why it is important that this desire be able to manifest itself in the presence of people who know something about what attracts the young person. Such people stand up for the youngster, assure him of the validity of his vocation, and by accepting him among them, signify to him that his desires, up to now only imaginary, can become a creative reality.

At the age of twelve, at Passover time in Jerusalem, Jesus separates from his parents for the first time.

He is called, and he answers. In the Temple he speaks and the learned doctors listen. He is busy with his Father's affairs.

Chapter III

LIKE A
LITTLE
CHILD

The Gospel According to Saint Mark
Chapter X, Verses 14 to 16

¹⁴ . . . "Let the little children come to me; do not stop them;
for it is to such as these that the kingdom of God belongs.
¹⁵ I tell you solemnly, anyone who does not welcome the king-
¹⁶ dom of God like a little child will never enter it." ·Then he
put his arms around them, laid his hands on them and gave
them his blessing.

The Gospel According to Saint Matthew
Chapter XIX, Verses 4 to 5

⁴ ". . . the creator from the beginning made them male and
⁵ female ·and . . . he said: This is why a man must leave father
and mother and cling to his wife . . ."

Gérard Sévérin

*Here children are put before us as models of life. Bet-
ter still (or worse still), Jesus invites each man to rediscover
the child in him so as to welcome the kingdom of God. This
is the requirement for living. There is no salvation outside
of this metamorphosis, it seems.*

*Doesn't psychoanalysis say, furthermore, that in order
to live we must "kill" both father and mother and that in
each one of us there is always a child to "kill" also?*

Françoise Dolto

To say that it is necessary to welcome the kingdom of
God as a little child is to say: "Let go your father and your

mother." This has the same meaning. This shortcut may appear to be abrupt, and yet . . .

When the little child is born, he does not yet have a father and a mother: he does not know them, they are not "co-born" with him. In order to survive, he must get along with the adults who are going to take care of him, protect him, raise him. But when he is born, does he have a father? Does he have a mother? Not yet.

The father and mother who engendered him have constructed him physiologically, but it is after his birth—sometimes long afterward—that, consciously or not, they will educate him, allow him to construct himself psychologically, day after day, with them as models, whether or not he receives, whether or not he perceives, their love or their indifference. He speaks the language that they understand, but as he grows more and more autonomous day by day, the child must abandon the upbringing that he has received from his parents in order to Be.

Do you mean that instead of being the object of the education offered by his parents, the child is going to become the subject of his own desires?

Yes, beyond his father and mother, who at first are models for growing up, the child will discover herself or himself becoming a woman or a man, as her or his parents have been in their time; like them, they have been conditioned by their own parents. They will then be able to discover themselves to be the child of God, precisely like their father and their mother and everyone who is human. If they let go of their father and mother, they will be able to discover their life—and the Life.

Often teachers or parents try, by giving life to chil-

dren, to give them their life-style, their frames of reference, their own methods as well. The child ends by confusing his life project with scaffolding, direction and signals, enthusiasm, ardor, passion, and conditioning—the mere wrappings!

Parents, schoolteachers, no matter how well-intentioned, cannot do otherwise than to guide children according to their own way of living, of seeing, of feeling. That is conscious on their part. What is more, whether or not they have desires to educate children, unconsciously they are examples, despite themselves. That is an integral part of education, of apprenticeship. It is sensually and psychologically human. Certainly, it is not spiritual.

We must rediscover the source of ourselves—that is to say, we must become both our own father and our own mother and therefore our own child. Thus, after having inevitably passed beyond being this or that parent, elder, or master, we are obliged to invent ourselves.

Let each person become the artist of what he has received!

The child who is born viable possesses everything that is necessary for him to live, but in order to survive and develop until he reaches the point of being an autonomous, social, responsible being, he needs aid, examples, guidance. He needs others. For his growth and his development he needs material aid, language, the support of those who are around him and who love him, who inform him—but also in some way deform him if he does not escape from this education.

Christ enjoins the person who has reached the age of reason and acquired grace in the eyes of this human mother and this human father to leave them and to rediscover, vis-à-vis God, that total openness which was his at the beginning.

This confidence that the child reveals to his parents is that which the Gospel arouses in us by the example of the life of Jesus.

Jesus is a path, nourishment, love, compassion, comfort in the worst moments of solitude and suffering, as parents once were to their child.

He therefore invites us to rediscover our principle, our home, the naïve and awakened source of our first youth, every day.

Jesus magnifies the natural power and knowledge of childhood. Doesn't "Let the little children come to me" mean "Let your children come to their freedom"? That is to say, "Do not block the momentum that takes them toward an experience for which they feel a call. Have faith in the life that animates what attracts them; do not stand in the way of their desire for autonomy. Let each little child come to say 'I'—not 'I-my-mama,' 'I-my-papa,' 'I-my-pal,' but simply 'I.'"

But what is this "I"?

To me this grammatical "I" is focused on a synthesis in progress, a felt cohesion, there, in our body, a place where time and space intersect, in the face of all the others: the "you's," familiar and formal, the "we's," the "they's," masculine and feminine. Christ is "I," the model of all those who say "me" and then "I" and thereafter feel spiritually called to the Truth that calls to every man, that calls him beyond words to the Word of his being, as a participant in God.

When he says, "Let them come unto me," that is the

same for him as saying, "Let the children come to *ME,* who am an *I*."

And like "I AM" and like "ME, I AM I," that is the same as saying "I AM," the son of "I AM."[1]

So let each child come to terms with BEING, being human, from day to day, from minute to minute. This is the permanent present, individualized in the masculine or in the feminine as each one of us is conceived.

Every person bears within himself the intuition of this eternal creation in the present, this Word made present in the incarnation of each and every one, the Word incarnate in our genetic, ethnic, individual linguistic particularities.

Instead of this identification with our parents, those adults who are our procreators, and instead of this emotional, temporal, sensual dependence on them, there is the pure desire to be. Beyond the Having, Knowing, Being Able To, whose uses and misuses are taught by the adult generation, there exists the desire for Being.

It is from a rupture of the parental zone of influence that freedom arises in the invention of Desire by the generation of sons and daughters—a race or a leap that seems imprudent, especially to parents. Trapped as they are in their role of those who are coresponsible for the body of their child, they also believe that they are justified in guiding his Desire.

A race or an imprudent leap to which Christ draws him or her who is attracted by his summons!

In fact, Christ does not guide but rather attracts us to him. Christ does not command; he calls.

You repeat here a favorite theme of yours: parents

---

[1] "I AM" being the name of God in the Old Testament, God names himself, in effect: "I AM THAT I AM." (Exodus III: 14; John VIII: 24)

should not keep their children dependent upon them through possessiveness or moralizing.

But Christ said this before me. One must leave one's father and mother! This is not a subject that is first and foremost one of my favorites—it is a fundamental principle set forth in the Gospel.

"Let them come to me, let them desire who 'I AM.' It is in their desire to come to me that they will find their truth, their path." And each one will become, called by the Word, which he symbolized on the day of his conception, an object of the subject of the verb To Be, as an object of "I Am." Beyond his name and his surname, each one will be nominative: the subject and the object of his truth on the march, of his truth that is becoming.

But all this is experienced by any human being. The carnal begetter that a human father is, gives his child all the potentialities of Desire. The male and female procreators give the human ovum all the possibilities of Desire, but among these potentialities the teacher—the real father—and the educator—the real mother—give the child only those that they recognize in themselves, through a process of identification. What novelty does Christ contribute here?

When Jesus says "Let the little children come to me," it is not just anyone who is speaking—it is the Son of God. And he thus says: "Beyond the identification with your father and your mother, you must be initiated into your Desire with reference to God. Do not remain shut up in the desire that came from your parents as partial representatives of God for a time, that desire of your early childhood when you were physically immature."

And in fact, the parents do represent God to the child,

for the child is small and his parents are big. Because the child is a small mass, a part of a greater supportive mass, and because for him his parents represent the carnal adult model that he tries to equal.

Because of this carnal dependence, the child may believe that the adult human being is the very representative of Desire, whereas in fact the parents are representatives only of the law of Desire in the ethnic group to which they belong. The growing child can persist in the belief that his father and his mother are materially the representatives of God. That is warped thinking.

Christ saying, "Let the little children come," in fact says, "These children do not belong to you; they belong to me, the Son of God; they are like me, children of God who have been made flesh through your mediation. You are children of God like me, having been made flesh by the mediation of your parents, themselves children of God. They are your equals before God.

"Let them come to the freedom of their Desire which God upholds." That is all.

So then, from the moment that a being focuses his love on Christ and what he says, he enjoys every freedom?

Yes, but what a scandalous piece of advice for us human parents, attached by all the fibers of our being to our children and them to us: letting them take risks that fill us with anguish! And for them, distressing their parents, bringing on their disapproval!

A child knows very well that it is through his father and mother that he has known love and security. So now he is no longer going to seek these life values in the person of his parents but in Jesus.

Who in our day would dare to say this to his child?

Chapter IV

CANA

The Gospel According to Saint John
Chapter II, Verses 1 to 11

1   Three days later there was a wedding at Cana in Galilee.
2 The mother of Jesus was there, ·and Jesus and his disciples
3 had also been invited. ·When they ran out of wine, since the
   wine provided for the wedding was all finished, the mother of
4 Jesus said to him, "They have no wine." ·Jesus said, "Woman,
5 why turn to me? My hour has not come yet." ·His mother said
6 to the servants, "Do whatever he tells you." ·There were six
   stone water jars standing there, meant for the ablutions that
   are customary among the Jews: each could hold twenty or
7 thirty gallons. ·Jesus said to the servants, "Fill the jars with
8 water," and they filled them to the brim. ·"Draw some out
9 now," he told them, "and take it to the steward." ·They did
   this; the steward tasted the water, and it had turned into wine.
   Having no idea where it came from—only the servants who
   had drawn the water knew—the steward called the bridegroom
10 and said, "People generally serve the best wine first, and keep
   the cheaper sort till the guests have had plenty to drink; but
   you have kept the best wine till now."
11   This was the first of the signs given by Jesus: it was given
   at Cana in Galilee. He let his glory be seen, and his disciples
   believed in him.

Gérard Sévérin

*At the marriage feast in Cana, Jesus is thirty years old.
He is a carpenter. At the marriage feast in Cana, two spouses
build their home and set their seal on their hearth.*

Françoise Dolto

That is quite correct; Jesus shows himself in Cana to

be the builder of another house, a spiritual house. Moreover, it is there that he experiences a decisive change.

This is first of all a human marriage feast: a young man and a young woman pledge themselves to each other before witnesses.

They exchange mutual love vows as they put their families and their individual pasts behind them.

At their wedding feast, they break away from their protected youth.

They call upon the energy of their ancestral lines through their desire, attracted as they are to each other, with the approval of their families. It is a deliberate, individual, familial, and social act.

They found a new, responsible, and generous social cell in a reciprocal total gift that gives meaning to their short mortal lives.

For all the participants, whatever their sex and their age, this young couple, on the day of their wedding, incarnate the past or future image of their dreams of their destinies. And so, let the magical and luminous juice of the vine flow freely!

Why magical, why luminous?

Because intoxication experienced in common offers a possibility of leaving reality behind and rejoicing together. This joy is also what redeems intoxication. And I shall add that the unconscious reveals itself then . . . *in vino veritas!*

Does getting drunk alone have another meaning?

Certainly. He who drinks alone shuts himself up. He fears leaving tangible reality behind in the company of others. He can exchange ideas with others only if he is sober, and therefore he can communicate only what is rational, judicious, sensible, reasonable. Everything outside of this category is the desert for him.

At Cana the opposite is true.

The pure water that the servants bring in the jars changes into a fermented drink, a source of laughter, of the forgetting of one's troubles and cares of every day. It is the milk of happiness that animates the feast in the souls of the wedding guests, that makes smiles flower, that allows the guests to pick the ripe grapes of fleeting fantasies with an intoxicating savor. When imbibed by many, this heady juice of the vine loosens tongues and hearts.

And it is this wine that Jesus will serve himself at another repast . . .

Yes, on the eve of his death, at his farewell meal, it is wine that he will consecrate as the living reality of his blood, that blood of the New Covenant.

In Cana, through the gift of a vegetable blood for a carnal wedding feast, for a human alliance, he begins his public life. In Jerusalem he will end his life by the gift of his carnal blood, for a spiritual wedding, a new covenant between men and God.

Let us examine this first miracle now, this first "sign" that Jesus makes. He works this miracle at the behest of his mother. Something important happens between this son and his mother! "My hour has not come yet," he says, and yet in the end this hour arrives. What is happening here?

What happens is a birth!

A wedding feast risks ending too soon: there is no more wine. Mary says to Jesus, "They have no wine." And what does Jesus answer her?: "My hour has not come yet." Whereupon Mary does not say: "Very well, then. His hour has not yet come." On the contrary she says to the servants: "Do whatever he tells you," as though she had not heard Jesus' words.

But what has she understood from what he says, to give signs of such assurance?

She has understood that by expressing himself in these words, Jesus is resisting being born to his public life because he is feeling anxiety.

In fact, Jesus is a man, and man experiences anxiety when faced with important acts wherein his destiny and his responsibility are at stake. Later, in the Garden of Gethsemane, he will weep, he will sweat blood, he will say that he is sad unto death.

In Cana, Jesus feels anxiety. Mary is less anxious than he; that is why her presentiments are correct.

Jesus is about to leave behind a life of silence, a hidden life, and embark upon a public life. This change of life is the cause of great anxiety.

For her part, Mary knows that his hour has come, in precisely the way a mother knows that her hour has come, knows that she is about to give birth.

Isn't Jesus' reply negative? Isn't saying "My hour has not come yet" a polite way of saying "No"?

Not at all. It is not a negation; it is a denial.

In fact, as you know, there is no negative in the unconscious. Hence, if Jesus answers, it is because at some level within himself he has "heard" his mother's request. If he answers by a denial, it is because he is anxious, and Mary has perceived his anxiety, which is witness to a desire.[1]

What does she understand by his question: "Woman, why turn to me?"[2] Why does she speak with such quiet authority to the servants, despite her son's verbal negation?

She is sure of the power that this prodigious man is about to exert, a power perhaps still unknown to him until he is thus pressed by her words.

But . . . where do Mary's words come from?

That is a question I am still asking myself . . .

Does Mary really realize the dynamic impact of her words when she states, "They have no wine"? Is this feminine intuition? A subtle or an unconscious pressure? A foreknowledge of the time that is at hand?

In fact, nothing is logical here. Mary asks for nothing and yet Jesus answers, "No." The simple words "They have no wine" become an order for the son. And what sort of a guest is this who gives orders in a house that is not hers? Who has caused her to speak in this way? Why do the servants heed her order?

Yes, from what level of her being has Mary said to her son, "They have no wine"? And to the servants, "Do whatever he tells you"? Does she not prove herself the initiator of Jesus' first steps in his public life?

Everything may seem so simple at the beginning, like everything that is really important—a banal reflection pro-

[1] This way of expressing one's anxiety, by saying the contrary in order to choke it back, occurs every day in an analytic cure, as it does in daily life. When someone says, for example, "I hope I'm not asking an indiscreet question, but how much money do you make?" he reveals that he is indiscreet by his very attempt to deny it.

[2] The King James Version here is "Woman, what have I to do with thee?" (*Translator's note.*)

nounced as a factual statement perhaps: "They have no wine." And yet . . . This story presents us with questions on every hand. This is because it is fraught with meaning.

Did Mary have any precise intention? Did Mary voluntarily take the initiative? Or did Jesus, by these everyday words, hear and recognize the sign from the Holy Spirit that he was waiting for, did he identify this as a message from his Father to manifest publicly the power of his creative word?

It is at Cana that the Gospels show us Mary speaking to her son and acting for the last time from this unique and mysterious position as an initiator.

It is now by other people, by the servants of the master with all their weaknesses, that Jesus will be roused to action.

Do you believe that Mary knows the role that she plays at this wedding feast?

I really don't know . . . I believe that she is necessary but I also believe that she is totally open and that she speaks out of sympathy: if wine is missing, won't joy be missing too? Without knowing it, in a very natural way, she is preternatural.

In the light of reason, in fact, nothing about Mary's behavior at Cana is logical . . . and yet it works!

In the end she speaks on one plane and the action takes place on another! This entire story and this dialogue might well make us believe that we're confronting a language of the deaf!

It is a little like what happens in psychoanalytic sessions. Something like a language of the deaf does in fact exist. One says something and, thanks to this language, something else is said in reply.

I find it interesting, when one reads the Gospel as a psychoanalyst, to see how, with denials as the point of departure, one ends up with light and the Christ, who is a man, passes by way of this psychological labyrinth where "no" means "yes" and vice versa. This is not lying, but rather a sign of anxiety within the birth process of a desire, which never occurs in a rational way.

If Jesus had not "heard" the words "They have no wine," he would not have answered and Mary would have understood that this was not the right moment for him to hear something on the subject.

Hence, Mary waits for him to be born to social life, and it is astonishing to see how something in Jesus still resists manifesting itself.

"My hour has not come yet."

"Do whatever he tells you."

You must understand that it is the strength of Mary that has given birth, phallically, if you'll permit me the word, to Jesus, through an act of power.

Jesus says: "What wouldst thou have me do, woman?"[3] I have always heard these words explained as the equivalent of "Why, woman, are you interfering in my affairs?" But as I see it, this means: "Woman, what is it that I suddenly find within myself? What is this extraordinary resonance that I hear in your words?"

It is a question. Christ asks his mother a question exactly as the fetus asks its mother a mute question at the mo-

---

[3] The reader is again reminded that the King James Version of this question of Jesus' reads: "Woman, what have I to do with thee?" This translation is closer to the French version of the Bible that Madame Dolto is commenting upon here. (*Translator's note.*)

ment when it first kicks in the womb, so that the mother says: "Ah, there, so a child is going to be born, is it?"

The same thing happens at this moment between Jesus and Mary: "Woman, why turn to me?"

Between a mother and her son, between a mother and her living fruit, which her child represents, this complicity is certainly present, and there is something that should not pass unnoticed: this is the moment when both reach a tacit agreement in order that a mutation, a birth, may take place.

Perhaps it is at this moment, at the marriage feast at Cana, that Mary becomes the Mother of God.

Chapter V

AT THE FOOT OF THE CROSS

The Gospel According to Saint John
Chapter XIX, Verses 25 to 27

[25] Near the cross of Jesus stood his mother and his mother's
[26] sister, Mary the wife of Clopas, and Mary of Magdala. ·See-
ing his mother and the disciple he loved standing near her,
[27] Jesus said to his mother, "Woman, this is your son." ·Then
to the disciple he said, "This is your mother." And from that
moment the disciple made a place for her in his home.

The Gospel According to Saint Mark
Chapter XV, Verses 33 to 37

[33] When the sixth hour came there was darkness over the
[34] whole land until the ninth hour. ·And at the ninth hour Jesus
cried out in a loud voice, "Eloi, Eloi, lama sabachthani?"
which means, "My God, my God, why have you deserted
[35] me?" ·When some of those who stood by heard this, they
[36] said, "Listen, he is calling on Elijah." ·Someone ran and
soaked a sponge in vinegar and, putting it on a reed, gave it
him to drink saying, "Wait and see if Elijah will come to take
[37] him down." ·But Jesus gave a loud cry and breathed his last.

Gérard Sévérin

*At Cana it is "glory" . . . At the foot of the cross it is
abandonment . . .*

Françoise Dolto

Poor woman! Truly, she stands there like all women
who have placed their hope in the success of their child,
and, lo and behold, in their eyes this child fails completely!

Jesus fails as a son, as an affective and carnal child. He realizes that she is suffering too much, that his mother is lost. If he disappears, she has nothing more to live for.

According to you, who will sustain her desire to live and the meaning of her life as a mother, now that her son, who had held such brilliant promise, is disgraced and is dying?

At Cana, it was a question of power. Here it is distress that comes to the fore. Mary needs a son in order to remain a mother. That is why Jesus gives her John. "Since you need a son, here he is."

For women have something like a carnal destiny to bear children. They also need a living being to love in order to continue to exist.

Does he feel pity for her?

Not at all. He pities neither her nor himself, the cause of her grief. He does not say to her: "Oh, poor Mother, how it hurts me to hurt you," as in pathological loves between son and mother, between mother and son.

He recognizes that it is in her role of woman as mother that she is suffering; this woman can no longer exercise her motherly function, and the motherly function lives by having living children: one of them dies, another is given to her.

He therefore offers her the means to bear and to accept her trial, which for a mother remains the greatest of all possible trials. A mother loses a part of her body, so to speak, in losing her child.

But with the loss of Jesus, Mary also loses any reason to hope.

Jesus gives her John, who becomes a substitute for himself as a son: "He will do for you everything that a son would do. And you will do for him everything that a mother would do for a son. You will be everything for him that a mother is and represents. And likewise he will be your son."

Thus, in her distress, he gives her human consolation.

But even so, John is not Jesus. He cannot replace her true son Jesus in her mother's heart.

No, of course not. And Mary suffers from this separation; she experiences a great inner abandonment. But Jesus tries to comfort her in her sorrow and shows us how we can console others.

As humans, we are all beings with ties, as far as our flesh is concerned, and beings possessed of speech, as far as our heart is concerned. Our desire is to communicate.

But when a being is no longer there and you miss him, this relationship is broken. Here Jesus offers John to Mary so that a tie between her desire to be a mother and an adolescent may survive. And he accompanies this gift with words: "Woman, this is your son."

It is thus that he creates a new vital relationship by means of words. These words are full of meaning in the context of Mary's desire to be a mother.

This desire does not die so long as a tie to another keeps it alive. When a tie has disappeared or has broken, one can create, with a word, a new vital tie.

What a vital link exists between Mary and John since they will speak together of Jesus! It is the name of Jesus that will unite them.

A few moments after having created this new tie between his mother and John, Jesus experiences doubt . . .

After his mission was accomplished as was written, doubt causes Christ to be gripped with anxiety, as every human being is, concerning his own faith, his certainty that he is in the right, that his desire is true, and that his work is accomplished.

But for Jesus here, it is not a question of a possible disappointment. His cry is that of desolation, the lapsing into a state of utter loneliness.

So long as he does not have human respondents or at least one single friend to justify him, every man may fall into a state of despair. He may then doubt his own validity, the validity of his desire and that of his acts.

Jesus lives this anguish in solitude, where there is no longer an echo, no longer a mirror, no longer any recourse.

His cry, "My God, my God, why have you deserted me?" redeems all our doubts concerning our desire, our vocation, our mission, the meaning of our life when we vacillate, swinging between the attraction of peaceful repose and the call to fulfill ourselves even though this may involve the voluntary risk of death.

After this appeal to God that God leaves unanswered, that arouses nothing but the mockery or the pity of men, Jesus moans in thirst like a man, like the being he was, with needs . . .

But it is at this moment that he shows himself to be different, to have come from elsewhere: in one last effort, expressed by a great cry, this dying man breathes a breath that comes from someplace else. Through this breath that he has lived and spoken and through this cry that he breathes, he goes beyond his passage in the flesh.

This long cry of Christ, abandoned by men, abandoned by God his Father, this cry that calls out with no audible answer—isn't this cry the model for the words of love, of love and desire at the very limits of articulation and sound?

It is by a cry that the newborn baby calls to its mother in order to snuggle in her arms, to calm himself, to quench his thirst and satisfy his hunger.

It is by a cry that every child calls to his father to be protected from the wicked.

It is by a cry that every human being calls out to preserve his right to physical integrity when some part of his body, betrayed by pain, escapes the cohesion of the whole and falls to pieces. This is a cry, then, for the help of another, for another's aid.

A cry of need, a cry of desire, a cry of love betrayed, a cry of a son of man, a cry of all men. They can all recognize themselves in his cry.

This cry, understood by all witnesses, this strange, mysterious, inexhaustible cry—is it not a message in which we can decipher the resurrection of the flesh, in which its promise becomes audible at the moment of Jesus' death on the cross?

This cry of Jesus, hanging there, naked, between heaven and earth, has been broadcast in space. Its echo can still be heard.

Chapter VI

RESURRECTIONS FROM THE DEAD

Foreword

Françoise Dolto

What a surprise I had, as a twentieth-century reader, on discovering the simple stories of the three resurrections! And naturally, my psychoanalytic training revealed an unexpected side of them.

Today, these Gospel stories tell us, first, about the imperious necessity of favoring the opening out and blooming of desire. Second, they show us that there is a dialectic founded upon the desire of a man and the laws that govern him.

In effect, the newborn baby is powerless to survive alone. He has need of nourishment, of protection, of the guidance of adults. But, at the same time, the newborn baby (and then the child) is informed, deformed, weakened, or supported in his natural intuitions by these adults.

He is thus unable to express his own desire in its totality, subjected as he is to the law of adults and the law of his unconscious. His desire has a life of its own. The laws of the unconscious have a life of their own. From them come the laws of the unconscious of those surrounding him. There is, therefore, such a thing as a dialectic—that is to say, a dynamism—that is continually evolving, continually bringing desire and law face to face.

I shall add that language has a privileged place in this evolution. It is through language, in the widest meaning of the term—that is, every mode of meaningful expression— mimicry, gestures, tones of voice—that the child opens himself to its being as a human creature and makes its masculine or feminine desire specific.

If language and desire are two of the elements that

constitute the person, the alienation from the law also appears to be necessary for one to live in society.

Is it not alienation that allows for the cohesion of human societies? Does not alienation also support technical and cultural creations, which are the regulators of society, before they become a source of crisis of dissociation, of disintegration? Without alienation, without submission to a law, no social life at all is possible.

Gérard Sévérin

Could you give a further explanation of how you understand the term "alienation"?

At one time, the concept of alienation, of someone who is alienated, described beings who were dangerous, irresponsible, or weak. Today we are discovering that these alienated beings (who are now more often called "psychopaths") have a behavior that results from an adaptation of their unconscious to that of others. Vital[1] and symbolic[2] processes can bring on an alienation that is an adaptation to the code of everyone else and not in conformity with their own desire.

Their behavior has a meaning. These ways of behaving thus have the value of a language. It is a question of decoding what they mean, of re-establishing in clear language what was not expressed, understood, or heard when the mental difficulty emerged.

Thus, in your view, there are two sorts of alienations:

[1] Accidents, illnesses, infirmities, and so on.
[2] Mourning, separation, precocious emotional overexcitement, and so on.

one which is not adapted to conventions and rules and an-
other which is adapted. Alienation is therefore subjection to
a law, a "belonging" to an authority?

Yes, one can say that, on condition that the adjective
"unconscious" is added to the words "belonging" and "authority"; that is correct. But the so-called alienated person
suffers from an alienation, I repeat, that is not in conformity
with the code that is generally accepted by all. He does not
understand them, he is no longer understood by them. He is
nonetheless a man for all that, a man of needs and desires.

At the same time, I shall add that without alienation
no communal life is possible. But though desire can be organized or channeled for a time, it cannot be so in a
definite, fixed, or stationary way. Desire cannot be im-
mobilized, and hence at a certain moment it is going to
overturn the law, shake certainties to their foundations,
delineate in another way the field of securities, and then
give rise to a new law, a new alienation which, in turn, aided
by a crisis . . . et cetera.

And this dynamic between desire and law can be
found in the Gospel stories of resurrections.

The Raising of the Son of the Widow of Nain

The Gospel According to Saint Luke
Chapter VII, Verses 11 to 16

¹¹ Now soon afterward he went to a town called Nain, accompanied by his disciples and a great number of people.
¹² When he was near the gate of the town it happened that a dead man was being carried out for burial, the only son of his mother, and she was a widow. And a considerable number
¹³ of the townspeople were with her. ·When the Lord saw her
¹⁴ he felt sorry for her. "Do not cry," he said. ·Then he went up and put his hand on the bier and the bearers stood still, and
¹⁵ he said, "Young man, I tell you to get up." ·And the dead man sat up and began to talk, and Jesus gave him to his
¹⁶ mother. ·Everyone was filled with awe and praised God saying, "A great prophet has appeared among us; God has visited his people."

Françoise Dolto

In this story Jesus sees the crowd of women who are weeping and men who are moaning about a bier on which a young man is lying. His mother follows, overwhelmed with sorrow. She is a widow who has no family. Jesus approaches.

What do the mourners say amid their sobs? What do these faces filled with consternation murmur? "It is her only son, her boy who is dead, her family support." "He was her cane on which to lean in her old age." "Misfortune has dogged her footsteps, for she is already a widow." "The poor woman, has God no pity?" "Who can bear to see such pain?" "Her little one has been taken from her by death." "What is going to become of her. She has nothing left . . . it is as though she were childless again!"

Jesus is moved by compassion. "Do not cry," he says to the woman. He approaches, touches the bier, and the bearers stop.

When we read this text today, we can imagine the shocked astonishment of this woman, of this mother. Her face is tense. Her eyes, in which an entirely new expression appears, are no longer bathed in tears, drowned in tears as they were a few moments before, and are once more in the shadows of her heart.

A frown appears on her face. She stares at this man who is disturbing the customary unfolding of the scene in which she plays her important and pitiful role of a tearful mother. Halting in her tracks, she stretches her head and her neck toward the man who has spoken; she says nothing, waiting for this strange turn of events to continue its course.

In the lived reality of this scene, there is a moment that is fantastic.

Gérard Sévérin

You have just recounted what the reader can imagine.

Yes, on reading this text of the Gospel, one can imagine the scene.

Wouldn't it be of interest to remain close to the text, to the symbolic level, without adding something that is imaginary?

Perhaps we don't have the right to extrapolate through

imagination and ought to confine ourselves to what the words say. But I know that everything that we read, everything that is said in words, has an echo that touches our entire being. And if we thus set aside the imaginary, we set aside our body and our heart as we abstract the message that the Gospels bring.

What is the relationship of words, thoughts, and the imaginary?

Though thinking or reflecting is not due to the imaginary, it is also true that thinking is not unrelated to the imaginary.

Beginning in our childhood we also apprehend the world that surrounds us by means of the imaginary; we people it with imaginary beings. And then we discover that the world is never what we imagine it to be.

The reality of the world is revealed when we collide with it, when there is a shock, a rupture, a breaking apart. We are then aware that the world is never what we imagine it to be.

In other words, we cannot approach, we cannot grasp reality directly. We can unite with it only through mediation, through the intermediary of the imaginary. There is no way of sparing ourselves this mediation.

It is certain that for each one of us, thinking, speaking, and imagining are parts of our being, of our life. Our imaginary constructs are part of us. It is with their aid then that we must approach, that we must grasp the reading of the Gospels.

But then . . . the ideal would be to have . . . evangelical hallucinations!

No, of course not. When my imaginary constructs meet with reality, as I have just said, a phenomenon of rupture, a gap, is produced. I am therefore obliged to depart from my imaginary constructs, my reveries, my illusions, because I am confronted with the sudden intrusion of reality, which is the cause within me of a separation that enriches me. Hence I, who am a woman, project myself more easily into this woman who undergoes a castration, a separation, a rupture that she refuses to accept and that she seeks to replace by all the social "business" of a funeral that makes her the object of everyone's pity.

Everything considered, the reading of the Gospels is a projection; that is to say, a scene described in the Gospels gives you the possibility of attributing your feelings to one or two persons and hence, perhaps, of understanding yourself better.

Yes, you are right, I imagine the scene as though I were there. This imaginary construct, which is that of the reader that I am, does not imply that everyone is going to have the same imaginary constructs that I do. But I believe that what is unique about biblical texts is that each one of us can project his imagination into them in order that the symbolic message may reach him.

If the symbolic message contained in the words comes through without there being a participation of our being and therefore of our body and the lived experience of each one of us, I think that in that case these texts do not bring life to our bodies, our minds, our hearts.

What the message of Christ says to us is that all his

words must be incarnated, must take on flesh, and must do so down to the level of the incomplete drives.[1]

Whatever his age, whatever his desire, his level of suffering and his psychic evolution, each person can project himself. The key to the reading of the Gospels is that it is necessary to project in order to receive.[2]

If one receives without having projected any part of his imagination, it is a false receiving. It is the receiving of an intellectual. The life-giving content, the change-effecting content, of the words of the Bible is deprived of avenues that can channel the creative effect within the reader.

According to what you say, it is not enough to project oneself into a scene of the Gospel; it is not enough to imagine; there must also be a fruitful response or clash, or a fertile fracture as well.

The arrival of Christ, for example, makes me think: "Why is he interfering like that? Why is he intervening in a

[1] When a person desires to communicate with another person, his desire passes through the intermediary of the incomplete drives—seeing, touching, hearing, etc. Desire passes through the medium, through the interpretation, of those parts of the body that have either a direct or an indirect contact with other persons through language.

These drives toward desire give pleasure. Sight, hearing, touch, each give partial pleasure. One speaks in this regard of "partial desire" for "partial pleasures." And one speaks of total desire for the total contact with another.

Thus in the Eucharist, one encounters a total person, and at the same time this encounter nourishes our partial impulses away from hunger, thirst, eating, drinking . . . oral, cannibal impulses, but not only that—also a desire that aims at a having, a taking, a knowing, a power, etc.

[2] Matthew V: 25–34. The example of the hemorrhaging woman demonstrates this. Jesus is jostled; people wanted to touch him but only one person projected her desire on him. It is by her alone that he was touched.

process that is all planned in advance where I, the wife-mother, have a role to play, where the son-corpse plays his role, and where in the final analysis everything is fine as it is?"

And here we see the truth of Christ coming to upset reality. I am in the act of imagining, I am in the act of conforming to a social process, and suddenly the real intrudes into reality; here are words that are absolutely surprising, unexpected, unusual.

It is the entire body of this woman, her whole being, that is overwhelmed by someone who violates the rules whereby a ceremony unfolds.

A man might see himself in the place of the dead boy . . .

He can project himself into the woman too, or he can project himself into the bearers. Why not put our projections into the reading of the Bible even while referring to the true text? This is something entirely different from the exegesis that seeks to establish the true text.

So for you the words matter very little; the important thing is what you put into them.

I don't say that they matter very little. It is necessary that the words remain the same in a text; it is the point of reference, the touchstone.

When he reads them, each person is going to live what he feels about them, but if each time that someone read a text, he modified the words of it, it would become just so much gibberish. One would have no text left at all. On the contrary, this text of the Gospels is capable of awakening a different imaginary construct in each person, according to what he has lived in his own life, and because this document does not change, it is a point of reference on which our imagination can project itself and against which it can collide.

Certain individuals read the Gospels from a "materialist" perspective.

Yes, and others from a "structuralist" perspective—why not?—but this is another sort of work. Each person, you know, has struggled against the nonfulfillment of his desire, each person has tried to fill the gaps in his hopes and thus possesses a fund of experience, that is, a culture, a knowledge, a technique. Each one is going to approach the texts of the Bible with his culture, with his capital of experiences, and on approaching them in different ways, what each one studies takes on a new meaning, and because the Spirit passes by way of this text, something new in him can be awakened.

Let us now go back to our passage of the Gospel.

The women friends on whom the mother leans no longer feel the weight of her body, which is entirely attracted toward the couple represented by Jesus and the corpse of her son. Her face is suddenly struck by the emotion of someone who, in the face of the intrusion of the totally unexpected, awaits the unimaginable. The crowd ceases its lamentations. Everything stops as though it were frozen.

In a natural voice, in the tone of a man who is speaking in the simplest possible way, Jesus addresses the figure lying there: "Young man, I tell you to get up." The dead boy immediately sits up, surprised at all this fuss, at all these people who are standing about, at this bier that he is sitting on. He looks around him in surprise. He sees his mother, whose expression reveals a face he has never seen before.

And who is this man standing next to him, who has just awakened him and brought him back from another world without knowing that the nothing that he is leaving behind goes by the name of death.

Whereas in his illness, his mind clouded with fever, he felt like a child who had forgotten how old he was, he awakens as a young man, through the effect of a man's voice speaking to his heart, telling him to rise.

What is this voice that is sweeter and stronger and also, in the secret of his being, more in accordance with his new desire, this man's voice which to his child's ear awakens the echo of the counsels and commands of his father who disappeared too early in his life? Is it he, risen from the dead, that he sees at his mother's side? I see her, out of gratitude, grasping Jesus' arm as it rests masterfully on the edge of the wooden cradle from which her thunderstruck son opens his eyes that are now those of a cured adolescent. Who is this man who has made this come to pass?

We are like the crowd of mourners, struck dumb with the truth that suddenly appears. We are like this dead boy restored to life. The meaning of what is happening still escapes us.

"Miracle!" one of the mourners close to the boy says. The crowd at the head of the funeral procession breaks up. Some people step backward in stupefaction, jostling those who step forward trying to see what is happening. There are young people who step out of the crowd and cry out and leap for joy, who are overwhelmed with emotion and grip their own clothes in the face of death which has let go of its prey.

Others are terrified and form little groups, shoulder to shoulder, staring at this spectacle, silent and tense.

Behind the group at the head of the procession, there are also people there who have come with the others, quietly chatting about their unimportant everyday affairs as they accompany the bier to the cemetery, as is the custom. Death is always disturbing, always unjust, especially premature death. It is better not to think too much about it, much less talk about it.

These people casually following the funeral procession are surprised at the interruption of their march amid the buzz of their voices and surprised at the breaking up of the group of those ahead of them. They look at each other, question each other. What is happening? Each of them seeks to read the answer to the enigma of this interrupted ceremony on his neighbor's face.

The news reaches them: the dead boy is alive.

"What was that you said? The dead boy is alive? What sort of nonsense is that?" They run back and forth, no one any longer certain of anything.

There are some who are irritated and leave, bursting out laughing. These are people who are upright, who want nothing to do with a bad farce or perhaps with a piece of sorcery that it is better to flee from and want to speak of something else, as a sign of denial or indifference.

In less time than it takes to tell it, each of them expresses his unbearable emotional tension in his own way. Disregarding custom, men and women walk over to each other and fall into violent arguments. Old people who are questioned murmur, "A sorcerer, sorcery, magic, Beelzebub," mingling together the idea of trickery and that of blasphemy. It is an attack on morality.

Delighted faces, hearts beating as fast as they can, joined hands raised toward heaven—faces too—as prayers are murmured. Women take each other by the arm and sing God's praises.

In this confusion, in this hubbub, in this emotional chaos, as the orange reflections in the sky announce that the sun is setting on the horizon, silence hovers over the arrested thoughts in the depths of hearts, murmurs stifle the words in people's throats. Sounds without words clash together, bringing to the ears of one and all the low murmurings of their blood and fragments of cries and exclamations to their lips.

Language has burst asunder in the face of this miracle that is an assault on death. It is complete regression.

Only the ritual of mourning is reassuring; in it the order of language is rediscovered. By repeating ritual words and gestures, the living help each other to separate themselves from the dead man who, when he was alive, was dear to them. (Flesh?[3] Yes, that too, through a subtle dialectic, in this case between a mother and a son.)

The man is there. The adolescent is fascinated by him. With his eyes fixed on the look in Jesus' eyes that speaks to his soul, he understands that he has just been delivered a second time, cut off forever from the magic dependence that bound him to his mother, to death.

A man's voice calls to him and directs the adolescent metamorphosis in his larynx and testicles. His desire is delivered from the fatal attraction to follow the path that has been dictated to him and instead to desert his home, his father who has died too soon.

His virility as a son which had been subservient to his father's power comes back to this boy who has been an orphan since childhood, whose mother had become his com-

[3] Dr. Dolto puns here on the French homonyms *cher* (dear) and *chair* (flesh); in the original text, moreover, the two words appear side by side to underline the pun. (*Translator's note.*)

panion and an orphan like himself. His option as an adolescent called to life sings of promises of love.

The order of desire, restored to symbolic life, has reached the group.

"Young man, I tell you to get up," Jesus says. The adolescent signals to the bearers—it is he who signals to the bearers!—who place the bier on the ground. And having taken on his full stature, the young man allows his joyous smile to beam, a smile that had been extinguished on the lips of the little sick boy that he once was, a boy who was passing life by to the point of dying.

For you, he was not dead, he was "passing life by"— that is, he was perishing because he was regressing in his relationship to his mother. He was therefore obliged to detach himself from her for a second time by freeing himself of her. But he could not do so without the intervention of Jesus, without this third summons that the man's voice represents.

Yes, that is precisely how it is.

On his feet, struck speechless for an instant, looking in turn at Jesus and his mother, he hesitates. Her eyes beseech Jesus to tell this son to come to her, so that she may embrace him, alive, and hold him to her heart.

The crowd, which had dispersed, has reassembled to see the dead boy rise. And now this crowd, silent still, draws away.

Astonished by his new view of the world, of women, the young man feels his heart and his blood palpitate at the sweetness of the young girls' cheeks, at their eyes gleaming with a fresh beauty. Mingling with the others, they form a circle around him, and to his fresh-blown smile, they are a promise of love.

I can see it. He walks back to the ramparts of his city. Young men of his age run forward, join together with him, and go off joyously singing Jesus' praises, to awaken the blasé hearts of upright people: "Hear ye, good folk, God has visited his people, the son who was dead is restored to life."

You seem to want to indicate that Christ resuscitates this child as a young man, and that even though he is given back to his mother, this child is no longer a child: he has become a son and an autonomous young man.

Jesus traced the point of no return for the shared fantasies of the mother and her child. This son had become twisted by his desire to please the woman who conceived and bore him; a desire which, perhaps, sustains the idea of duty he had received from others.

In the eyes of the crowd, wasn't the duty of this child to devote himself to his mother, for her purposes? He was obliged to be her cane on which to lean in her old age.

It is to his freedom as a man that this lucid, calm, firm male voice awakens him. Jesus awakens the future man in the child of a dead father, and along with awakening him to manhood, he awakens him to his lineage, to his fertile destiny. As he lies dead, Jesus tears him away from the call that he has heard from his father. This father, whose voice had echoed in his ears in his early childhood, was his ideal self. Through death, by leaving his mother, it was his father that he was about to find.

A son always tries to imitate his father; a girl imitates her mother. That is why a male desire incited this young man to follow his father at the price of deserting his child's body burdened with a passivity that was sucking him down, as a parched tree is sucked down, in the sterile sand of a maternal and filial love that are infantile.

But in so doing he ran another risk. By being amenable to identifying with his father, the son was willing to die, to follow him in order to fight against the fact that he had remained a child coupled to his mother.

If I understand you correctly, what you are speaking of is the Oedipus complex. Does it appear to you that this child had been unable to come to terms with it, and because of the pathology of his family, he had remained erotically linked to his mother without knowing it?

Yes, the absence of his father to mediate between him and his mother had petrified his desire into impotence. Faced with his abandoned mother, guided and surrounded only by her, he was unable to achieve his procreative destiny, for, unknowingly, she was barring his way.

In effect, this son had to bind up her painful wounds, fill the void left in her heart by her husband, relieve the lack of tenderness that this woman no longer expected from any man. He alleviated his mother's distress as a woman by devoting himself to her; but his repressed genital desire kept him from having the joys and life project appropriate for his age. The confined atmosphere in which this son-mother couple lived had become morbid, and without their knowing it, the desire of both of them had become regressively incestuous.

To sum up: for this mother, who was a mother only once and deprived of the embraces of a spouse, her child was obliged to replace everything—the social, the erotic and the tender.

But this same thing happens even in our day. How many sons, of how many women without a man, are kept in the limbo of puerile love, sad and studious, the artificial consorts of a mother over whom they jealously keep watch like authoritarian guardians—sons barred from the desire appropriate to their age by their mother who stifles them with her excessive, paralyzing maternal solicitude.

Such women, still young, deaf to the calls of their own desire and blind to possible suitors, devote themselves to their widowhood and their sterility, considering it an admirable sacrifice! Concerned about the future of their sons, they are constantly on guard against the female bodies that pass too close to the territory they share with their sons. Greedy or flattering felines, they isolate and spin a cocoon around their chaste and neurotic sons.

How could such sons get away from such mothers? Society would stigmatize them as ungrateful.

If life calls these boys, if a virile desire awakens their nubile sexuality, the reproving gaze of their mother, the risk of her curse slyly descends upon them. They cannot venture outside the deadly, daily routine of their home. They can imagine only horrible or idealized sexual exploits. They calm their reveries through masturbation, which relieves their loneliness.

"Young man, I tell you to get up." Jesus gives back to this woman, who is herself drowning in despair, a son brought back to life, standing there before her. In his dual relationship to her, this son was arrested in the face of his puberty, with no promise of offspring, with no outlet for his desire as a man.

His life forces vanquished, slowly dying a symbolic death from day to day, his body could not help but be the prey to sickness or to abandonment to the refuge of sleep in order to forget his needs—to the point of physical death.

For you, Jesus of Nazareth recognized that beneath this petrified form a young man, supposedly dead, could live if he were separated from his mother.

Through his imperative, public summons, Jesus gives him the stature of a free man, which he reveals to him, and the momentum to construct his life in the face of a dumfounded society that he silences.

He awakens this youngster with an undeveloped heart to his bodily virility. Every boy is aware of this, because his sex organ is visible and its flesh becomes erect. But what can be done, when no man initiates you to the law of this flesh?

So you think that it is by the command "Young man, I tell you to get up" that Jesus frees this young man, not only of death but of his mother?

Yet the text does not speak of a separation from his mother; on the contrary, it is written that Jesus has compassion for this woman and gives her back her son.

In the story of the resurrection of the son of the widow of Nain, it is a young man and not a child that Christ brings back to life.

In his male voice he calls him, he names him, he declares him a "young man," and it is thus that he gives him back to his mother in accordance with the law of the castration of genital desire. This youngster is definitely embarked upon his adult life now. The young man lives. The child is no more.

Let us compare this story, as has always been done, with that of the resurrection of the son of the widow by Elijah. Already in I Kings XVII, we see that the law of the castration of desire is implied in the resurrection of this child.

This passage says that Elijah asks for asylum from a widow who lived with her only son, who was still a child. The three of them—Elijah, the mother, and the child—eat a meal together. Shortly afterward, the child is taken sick and dies. Believing herself to be punished for her sins, the widow calls upon Elijah.

Elijah separates the child from his mother. He takes him up into the upper room, a symbol of the allegorical ascension inherent in the growth of a child. In this upper room, Elijah stretches himself out on the child three times, praying God to give the soul back to this body.

For a psychoanalyst reading this story, these three contacts of a man lying stretched out on the body of a child symbolize the threefold initiation of the desire of the child into the legitimate patterns of desire of a man.

The first initiation is oral castration, that is to say, weaning—the first separation of the child's mucous membrane from his mother.

The second is anal castration, the separation of the child's "doing," having to do with his body and his voluntary motor system: he is no longer his mother's helper nor the executor of her desires.

The third separation is that of genital desire and the desire to have a child with the mother. This is the incest taboo.

These nonsexual contacts of Elijah with the body of this youngster symbolize the possible identification of a child with a man, thanks to the castration of libido at each of these stages of evolution. The young man enters into the pattern of desire in a man's body restored to its power by the transformation into legitimate patterns of the specific (Oedipal) taboo against oral, anal, and genital desire to covet the woman in the mother who bore him, nursed him, and raised him—the woman who is the wife of his absent father.

So, like the son of the widow of the Book of Kings, the son of the widow of Nain is a living young man, separated from the fantasies of his infantile sexuality, whom Jesus gives back to his mother, who is herself separated from him by the words of the man who brings him back to life.

Between these two resurrections there is a difference that is a major one. A psychodrama is played out with Jesus, wherein words do all the work of castration. It is not Jesus' body on the body of the other, as with Elijah—it is the word, which is efficacious and restores desire to its real meaning and place.

He does not use magic as Elijah does?

No, through him it is the irruption of the real, of the symbolic, of the imaginary in us: it is a sacrament.

That is what Jesus brings: the spoken word is the mistress of all desires when it is chaste and in the service of the desire for God in each one of us.

This seems to me to be the lesson given by Christ in the resurrection of a young man who was about to be buried because he had every appearance of being dead.

Let us note, furthermore, that Jesus does not attach this man to himself, to his humanity, in a parasitic way.

Jesus places his arm on the bier, that arm which the Holy Spirit makes athletic and imperious, on this bier on which all the mourners together, with tears and lamentations, are taking this adolescent who is asleep to his grave.

Jesus thus imposes on the mother the castration of her desire, and her son is thereby cured.

To sum up, the love of this mother is a perverse love, that is to say, a parasitical, misplaced love: her son was to remain the cane on which she would lean in her old age. He thus became a retarded child whose duty it was to share his mother's life to her declining days. She had annexed this child of hers. And so Christ brings about a separation.

If young people know that later they must aid their parents when these latter have become too old to continue to help themselves, they also know that in order to honor the life that has been given them by their parents, they must leave their father and their mother, they must go towards society, and at a distance from the paternal home and fireside, in order to take responsibility for their own femininity or masculinity upon themselves.

But very often children who have lost their father prematurely hear things like "Your poor mother . . ." and "My poor child . . ." as though, in the absence of the head of the family, strength had necessarily deserted both the mother and the children.

We are accustomed to this pathological pity, but we are not aware that it is harmful to the development of the child.

In fact, don't we often hear it said, "Since your father is dead, you are now the head of the family, your mother's support, think of her, replace your father"? These are corrupting words, for they are in the final analysis counsels to behave in a way that is imaginarily incestuous.

Might one not say, on the contrary, "Since your father is dead, you are now in charge of solving all the problems that arise. Now that your father is dead, your mother must continue to live, she must not be a burden either to herself or to society. You will help her by causing her the least possible work around the house, you will help her to work outside the home and to know that everyone hopes that she will remarry"?

In this story, which to our eyes, is illuminated by the discoveries of psychoanalysis regarding archaic sexual desire, Christ re-creates a trinitarian, or at the very least a triangular, situation, like that of the primitive procreative scene confronting every human being.

This passage from the Gospel teaches us that no human being can be an attribute, an object, or a submissive complement depending on another human being. He teaches us freedom.

In the eyes of the psychoanalytic reader of today, the son of the widow of Nain who is brought back to life bears witness to the inhibiting ravages of human desire when its momentum, both biological and emotional, is blocked.

Here the momentum is arrested by the widowhood of the mother, followed by the regression of her femininity. It is then that an imaginary, fetishistic tie with her son is formed: to her this child represents her strength, her power, the allurement of the symbolic phallus. Because the father was not able to take charge of separating his child from his mother, he was not able to take charge of the education of the sexuality of his son so as to lead him to the threshold of his genital sexual power.

That is to say, with such a mother and an absent father, there was nothing that stood as an obstacle to the imaginary ties that were awakened from the umbilical period.

These ties are slyly reconstituted between mother and son. With the pretext that she needs his vigilant protection, the mother attaches herself to her son. Their complicity, blindness, or cowardice gives their friends a clear conscience.

We know that this boy was an only son and being a Jew, was therefore circumcised.

This rite is important if it is explained by words from the father. In fact, circumcision marks every male baby's access to the society of men.

It is an allegory of the definitive quietus that the male gives not only to the placenta but to the enveloping protectiveness of his mother. The protective foreskin of the penis is an expression: "Not only have you left behind all protection as regards your body but also as regards your sex organ. You must accept the responsibility for yourself."[4]

Since this young man of Nain had no brother or sister,

---

[4] The problem is different for a girl. She must model herself after her mother, and it is only out of rivalry that she desires a man. She thus desires her father, but if the latter does not desire her and says to her, "You were not born for me," she is led to search for the substitute of the sex-organ of her father in another man. It is the father who is responsible for the desire or nondesire; it is he who unconsciously forms his daughter.

What frees the daughter is not the sexual act. Her partner can be lived as an imaginary betrayal of her mother, as a trap for her father. It is her first child that can free her completely by superceding her identification with her mother. It is her giving birth for the first time that makes a daughter a woman.

By having a child, she will perceive that he does not belong to her alone but also to the paternal line, to the line of her husband. She will then experience a transfer from dependence on her father to dependence on a man other than her father, and if she continues her unconscious libidinal evolution, she will even attain love without dependence, desire without allegiance.

and hence no rival, he did not have the experience of a new fertility of his parents after him. He had only this one mark of the initiatory separation of circumcision between himself and his mother. And if this mark has not been reinforced by a father's words, a child who has no rival in genital love (genital love that demonstrates that it is another sort of desire than that which he has for his mother) does not understand, through the sole power of his imagination, the difference between the genital desire of an adult and the pregenital desire of a child for his mother.

That is to say, then, the family situation of this young man of Nain could have been very difficult. He was an orphan without a father, and we have seen the many things that the absence of the father can bring about. And now you seem to be saying that being an only child can also bring on psychological difficulties.

Not having a brother or a sister who is younger is especially complicated. That is what the last child of a family always experiences. (The only child and the last child have more difficulty detaching themselves from their childhood.)

The boy formulates his question in more or less these terms: "Hasn't Papa become impotent after my birth?" And the girl: "Hasn't Mama become sterile?"

The child needs to experience his parents as people who are young, alive, dynamic. "Old" parents are not models. That is why it is important that children know that their parents are neither impotent nor sterile. And if they do not have another brother or sister, it is because their parents either do not desire to have any more children or else hope to have more.

Children experience themselves as rivals of their model

of genital life. This is a healthy and natural lever for their development.

Let us go back to this Gospel. If he was in good enough health, ought this boy from Nain to have fled and abandoned his mother?

Yes, of course he should have, but then he would have been accused of ingratitude by society.

He put his vigilance to sleep, he allowed himself to be subjugated by death impulses that prevail over the life impulses in the unconscious if, between early sexuality and puberty, any young boy or girl does not dare to take on the responsibility for the desire that calls him or her out of the family home; or if a perverted sentiment of filial duty keeps them from distressing anxious parents or from escaping from parents who are overly possessive or authoritarian. This son of a widow is the prisoner of this deathly conflict.

By letting himself die, this big little boy also commits, unconsciously, a double murder of his own person: that of the son who is the representative of his father and that of the future father that he was to be. A symbolic murder and a real murder.

He identifies with his father in death and removes himself from the unconscious lust of his mother and from his for her.

Instead of fleeing, he makes his escape through illness and death.

He could not leave his mother without someone's aid. The young man chooses death because in his unconscious death harbors the pleasure that would make him a rival of the father: he did as well as his father did—he knew how to die.

He copied the father he knew; he did not imitate what his father did when he was a young man, since, I repeat, in order to marry he would have had to leave his own mother and choose a woman outside of his family.

For this young man, illness and death likewise contained contradictory and complementary joys: without anxiety the unconscious satisfies the desire to have himself castrated by the jealous father: "Your scrotum or your life?" "Both, Papa! You will not have me alive but I will have you dead!"—that is to say, "Mama will think more of me than of you!"

This state of sleep that Jesus stigmatizes is a shying away from the law of honoring one's father and one's mother and oneself by honoring one's patronymic and by living one's genital desire with a person outside the family. In a word, by taking responsibility for the law of desire linked to love, outside the family.

I can see from here the reader's astonishment at this dialectic of the unconscious, and I will go so far as to say the Freudian dialectic of the unconscious. But for narcissistic neurotics, for example, the absurdity of death—as psychoanalysis has discovered—is no more fearful for the unconscious than life.

In point of fact, for the unconscious, negation does not exist. Death, the negation of life, is thus totally unknown to the unconscious. In any case, death can conceal the satisfaction of a desire, or, more exactly, death can offer the mirage or the trap of satisfying a desire when this desire cannot be experienced without guilt attached—that is to say, when the genital ethic is perverted.

Hence death is terrifying only for the conscious. May not death be only a conscious desire for an unattainable object?

It can also be the means to fulfill oneself through an imaginary return to the time before conception—to that nirvana that real death promises, it is believed, to our joyous fantasies. This nirvana would be, then, the return to the conscious nothingness that people wrongly imagine the paradise of the mother's womb to be.

Thus death can be glimpsed, not only as an eternal repose, but also as a means of receiving the punishment for genital desire forbidden by a castrating father.

In short, attracted by death, the young man who is nubile and not initiated into life may imagine that all his desires will finally be satisfied therein.

And the young man of Nain that the bearers are taking to the grave has every appearance of death. He is "going-toward-becoming death." There is no doubt that if he is buried, he will really be dead in the next few hours!

So he is not dead—he is "asleep," like Jairus' daughter or Lazarus?

Yes. He is in a state of apparent death—in a prolonged coma, as we would describe it today. His soul, as people say, has left his body before its time. It is a premature death in relationship to this boy's destiny. It comes too soon, as a result of the conditions of his upbringing. He lacks someone to keep his desire alive, a being to love in order to make his heart beat, a master to live by in order to awaken his mind.

For you, we are a body and a soul. If there is a separation, does it mean death?

If separation is prolonged, it means death. But in the beginning, it is a beginning of death; death is not always immediate or total.[5]

But where does this soul go?

What way is there to know! But despite our ignorance regarding this subject, we do have some idea of what the meaning of death is for those who are left behind.

For the social group at Nain, this death has become the hand of destiny, as the saying goes, and no more than a subterfuge of desire.

In his clear-mindedness, Jesus understands the situation. He makes himself the representative of the symbolic spouse and, at the same time, of the symbolic father, both of the woman and the boy. He restores them both to the life of desire, in their purified genital impulses, separating the two of them by his words. It is no longer a child but a young man who lives.

For Jesus is a "father"—"He who sees me sees the Fa-

[5] In our day, we know that the heart can cease beating though an electrocardiogram shows that the heart muscle is still alive. Likewise, if one follows the trace of an electroencephalogram, the brain can still be alive even in prolonged coma. These are cases in which attempts are made at resuscitation. Where is the soul in these states of apparent death?

The body is lying there, apparently a corpse. Only when the trace definitely flattens out is the person declared dead. Often, in the course of attempts at resuscitation, the trace flattens out after starting up again several times before definitely flattening out and thus ending all hopes for revival. Sometimes a person hovers for a long time in a state that is not yet death but at the same time is no longer life.

ther." He is the father of all humanity, that is—he is not the man, the husband of the mother, but rather we find in him the father, the paternal genius, the procreative essence.

He constantly offers birth, rebirth, resurrection, and life.

He continually topples us over from the field of the law into the field of desire.

Always, "with him, everything is new once again."[6]

[6] Olivier Clément, *L'Autre Soleil* [The Other Sun], Paris, Stock.

The Healing of the Woman with a Hemorrhage and the Raising of the Daughter of Jairus

The Gospel According to Saint Mark
Chapter V, Verses 21 to 43

21 When Jesus had crossed again in the boat to the other side, a large crowd gathered around him and he stayed by the lake-
22 side. •Then one of the synagogue officials came up, Jairus by
23 name, and seeing him, fell at his feet •and pleaded with him earnestly, saying, "My little daughter is desperately sick. Do come and lay your hands on her to make her better and save
24 her life." •Jesus went with him and a large crowd followed him; they were pressing all around him.

25 Now there was a woman who had suffered from a hemor-
26 rhage for twelve years; •after long and painful treatment under various doctors, she had spent all she had without being any
27 the better for it, in fact, she was getting worse. •She had heard about Jesus, and she came up behind him through the
28 crowd and touched his cloak. •"If I can touch even his
29 clothes," she had told herself, "I shall be well again." •And the source of the bleeding dried up instantly, and she felt in
30 herself that she was cured of her complaint. •Immediately aware that power had gone out from him, Jesus turned around
31 in the crowd and said, "Who touched my clothes?" •His dis- ciples said to him, "You see how the crowd is pressing around
32 you and yet you say, 'Who touched me?'" •But he continued
33 to look all around to see who had done it. •Then the woman came forward, frightened and trembling because she knew what had happened to her, and she fell at his feet and told
34 him the whole truth. •"My daughter," he said, "your faith has

restored you to health; go in peace and be free from your complaint."

35 While he was still speaking some people arrived from the house of the synagogue official to say, "Your daughter is dead: 36 why put the Master to any further trouble?" ·But Jesus had overheard this remark of theirs and he said to the official, "Do 37 not be afraid; only have faith." ·And he allowed no one to go with him except Peter and James and John the brother of 38 James. ·So they came to the official's house and Jesus noticed all the commotion, with people weeping and wailing unre- 39 strainedly. ·He went in and said to them, "Why all this com- 40 motion and crying? The child is not dead, but asleep." ·But they laughed at him. So he turned them all out and, taking with him the child's father and mother and his own companions, he 41 went into the place where the child lay. ·And taking the child by the hand he said to her, "Talitha, kum!" which means, 42 "Little girl, I tell you to get up." ·The little girl got up at once and began to walk about, for she was twelve years old. At this 43 they were overcome with astonishment, ·and he ordered them strictly not to let anyone know about it, and told them to give her something to eat.

Gérard Sévérin

Have you noticed that the Gospels never separate the story of the resurrection of Jairus' daughter and that of the woman with the hemorrhage?

Françoise Dolto

If these two stories are associated in the fabric of the Gospels, it is because they are linked by an unconscious organic and spiritual association of ideas. In fact, the two are one and the same story: there is a woman whose feminine destiny has been blocked and a man whose paternal destiny has become a false one.

A woman suffers in her femininity for twelve years, while a little girl twelve years old, even before she has become a woman, sees her destiny blocked.

For twelve years this woman with the hemorrhage has been excluded from the arena of sexually desiring and desirable women. A little girl of twelve dies instead of entering the age of nubility.

In fact, it is written that this woman has losses of blood, hemorrhages; when it is said that a woman has "losses of blood," it is usually because she has an excessively heavy menstrual flow. But here the word is more serious; it means a hemorrhaging woman.[1] These serious losses of blood have lasted for twelve years.

So this so-called impure woman is a tragic figure: she cannot have sexual relations with a man.

Listen to what the law decreed for this woman.

It is written in the Book of Leviticus (XV: 24–25): "If a man sleeps with her, he will be affected by the uncleanness of her monthly periods. He shall be unclean for seven days. Any bed he lies on will be unclean. If a woman has a flow of blood for several days outside the period, or if

[1] I shall here point out that I have not found the term "hémorroïsse" in dictionaries—a Greek-derived word often used in [French] translations of this passage. Because of its phonetic resemblance, we might be led to believe that this woman's trouble might have been bleeding hemorrhoids. But in my opinion this is not the case at all. Today this symptom would be called "metrorrhagia." (Metrorrhagia is profuse bleeding from the uterus, between normal menstrual periods. *Translator's note.*)

the period is prolonged, during the time this flow lasts she shall be in the same state of uncleanness as during her monthly periods." You can imagine what a tragedy this has been for this woman for twelve years.

By contrast, the daughter of Jairus would appear to have had a happy life.

Her father loves her. For twelve years she has been the pride and joy of those about her, of her family, and of people who have a certain reverence for her father, who is a local notable: he is an official of the synagogue.

But this father appears to be unconsciously and incestuously fixated upon "his" daughter. This father is a giant nursing baby clinging to the breast of his mother or grandmother, whom his daughter unconsciously "re-presents" to him. He keeps her "little" in his own sphere; without realizing it he wants her to be dependent on his possessive paternal love. Jairus does not mention his wife, the child's mother. That is really quite astonishing, isn't it?

Perhaps it was the custom in that day and age not to pay any attention to one's wife.

But if that is so, why is he concerned about his daughter? No, he presents himself as the only one sorely tried: "My little daughter," he says. He does not say: *"Our* daughter is desperately sick."

Do you think, then, that this father "possesses" his little girl?

Yes, but let us make sure that we agree on the meaning of the word "possesses."

It is not possession in the usual meaning of adult sexuality, nor is it a diabolical possession. What it is a question of, however, is the play of a desire that harms the psychosomatic wholeness of this child, that stands in the way of her freedom to live, preventing her from developing toward a liberation of her feminine powers as a young girl and of her ability to make choices beyond the paternal bosom. In psychoanalytic jargon, we might say that this is an overprotective father of the motherly type. He is animated by a possessive love for his daughter whom he calls "little" (she is twelve years old at the time of this story), a sign that he considers himself "big" as compared to her, and he does not talk of the mother of this child because he is unconsciously playing her role. He is not consciously aware of this.

After Freud, who discovered the confusion of love and desire, psychoanalysis has revealed to us the confusion of desire and need in the course of everyone's childhood. Hence, psychoanalysis permits us to understand what are called "affective fixations of a neurotic type" to human beings who are treated by us as "partial objects," belonging to a stage of pregenital sexuality. Their "possession" has become so pathologically part of our lives that we no longer recognize in these human beings their status as autonomous subjects.

The small child, of course, cannot be autonomous; he depends upon the adults who take care of him. But it often happens that these adults, for their part, enjoy this dependence of their children, and when these children grow up, the parents are unable to free them from this total subjection.

The children of these "devouring" mothers do not have the freedom to love other persons, to escape from these mothers' embraces, to hide the least thought from them.

A father can also be as "devouring"—that is to say, as moved by "oral" desire—as a mother.

Once the child has reached the age when he can follow his own initiatives—which represent no danger to the child—certain mothers and fathers do not tolerate such freedom of choice. Their authority over the child's every act and gesture literally imprisons him within a network of taboos on his freedom of conduct and makes him feel guilty if he risks violating them. Some of them become cases of "character disorder," others grow sickly.

In fact, these are parents who forbid their children the pleasures appropriate to their age, so that the children pay for any sort of enjoyment and every experience of freedom with guilt. Such parents act this way out of anxiety, and also out of jealousy. Their guidance overwhelms the child. He is their slave, compliant or rebellious, living uneasily and badly, incapable of assuming the responsibility for his nubility.

The daughter of Jairus has also been kept by her father, for twelve years, in the status of an object partly of a devouring love and partly of an infantilizing love.

Alone and without aid from outside her family, she cannot help but become devitalized. Her father loves her with a love that can only be called unconsciously incestuous, a libidinal love of the oral and anal type that makes her a prisoner in a golden cage.

So then, according to you, her death is provoked by the person who asks Jesus to cure her?

Yes, but thus far it is a question only of an apparent death. Christ himself says, quite correctly, that the young girl in this child is sleeping.

The father, too, as a man, is threatened by death; he is

ill, as is the woman with the hemorrhage. Christ takes pity on him. He immediately grasps the disorder of this father's paternal love—his deviancy, if you prefer—by losing his daughter, he does not lose his blood, as the woman did, but rather the fruit of his blood. He even forgets to mention his spouse, the mother to whom the child belongs as much as to him. He notices only his own suffering. His wife is not present in the words he speaks.

It is the only case in the Gospels in which a man goes out of his way on behalf of a daughter. One sees women, mothers, speaking to Christ of their children, but Jairus is the only man. His behavior must have made a strong impression on the Apostles.

But what sickness is this child suffering from?

Do you mean what are her symptoms?

The text does not say, but we understand from it that for twelve years this child has been sick from her femininity, that she has been artificially kept in an infantile position of dependence. She is a little cherished object, the affectionate kitten belonging to a man who is thinking only of himself when he asks Jesus to cure her.

His distress as a man who is rich but powerless moves Jesus, for Jesus always has compassion on our weaknesses. Given his character, Jairus cannot bear to have his little girl grow up, cannot bear to have her escape by becoming nubile and then a woman and a mother in her turn.

And is the same thing true of the woman with the hemorrhage?

In fact, this woman's body has attained its adult growth, but her blood flows uselessly, her feminine sexuality drains away and dies, outside the circle of desire and love; she cannot recognize herself as a woman in a man's eyes.

Not having entered the genital cycle, she lives in hiding and in need, like a sexless being. A woman who has not blossomed, she continues to have an issue of blood whose flow does not transmit life.

She is impure in her own eyes, she is impure in the eyes of men. Untouchable and frustrated, she has been in despair for twelve years, as the object of Jairus' despair, his daughter, is now.

Her sexuality which has been disturbed for twelve years tortures her; socially she is poor and humble. In the case of the father, it is his generative power that for twelve years has been his pride, along with his worldly wealth. And now he is the most miserable of men; his life is losing its meaning. And we see him become as humble as the poorest of men. He is now an authentic seeker of something.

Why, according to you, is there a miracle?

"If I can touch even his clothes, I shall be well again." And the source of the bleeding dried up instantly, and she felt in herself that she was cured of her complaint. Immediately aware that power had gone out from him, Jesus turned around in the crowd and said, "Who touched my clothes?" His disciples said to him, "You see how the crowd is pressing around you and yet you say, 'Who touched me?'"

Doesn't this mean that one can approach, touch, make contact, attain, but if the desire which is an appeal for living communication, which is a personal entreaty—if the desire is not embraced, has not become a life-project—one can receive nothing? Jesus himself cannot give his strength to all of those who press about him if they do not desire or ask with the authentic power of desire, which is a forgetfulness of self and total faith in the other, a unique desire borne by an immense hope, so that one forgets oneself in his total faith in the other.

It is the intention of the person who desires and the intensity of her entreaty alone which call forth Jesus' reply. This touching of Jesus' cloak is a form of prayer in action. Jesus, the source of a living power, answered it unconsciously, but felt that power had been taken from him.

"My daughter, your faith has restored you to health; go in peace, and be free from your complaint." Cured, she feels ashamed of having stolen power like a thief from this figure who can do everything. No, he says in essence, it is not I, it is yourself who has rediscovered through faith the law of your femininity.

Immediately after the flow of this woman's blood is stanched, the news reaches Jairus: "Your daughter is dead: why put the Master to any further trouble?"

Thus at the very moment that the adult woman cures herself, the little girl begins to die. There is an obvious link here. This child lived only in a state of negation, of a loss of desire. She was "vampirized" by the love of this father. This man had stifled every demand in her, every reason to live, for twelve years. Her father asks not to lose her, for she is his blood and, even more, she is his life. Furthermore, through her death her father has the revelation that she is the sole meaning of his life at the expense of the meaning of her own life for herself.

As you know, every little boy dreams of equaling his mother by giving birth, through his alimentary tract, to an offspring that will be all his own, a parthenogenic and sterile offspring, the object of his desire and his love belonging to him alone.

The daughter of Jairus is like this imaginary passive oral-anal image, a child with every possible material advantage whose desire has never been castrated: no one has ever refused her anything, she has never had anything either to demand or to do. The fetishistic phallus of her father, she has always been spoiled and cosseted. She had emptied herself, she was emptied of the strength that desires give as they push each one of us to seek to satisfy their demands.

If the child is separated from the help of the adult and his attentive care, he feels his desires and experiences their risks and thus forges his autonomy.

But why imagine that this little girl was spoiled and fawned upon in this way?

As I was saying, these two stories are, first of all, associated, linked in the Gospels. And then the same number of years: twelve is the number associated with miracles—twelve years of hemorrhaging for the woman, and of the girl we are told: "The little girl got up at once and began to walk about, for she was twelve years old."

Moreover, her father is surely well-off; he is an official of the synagogue.

And then, too, he is a man who goes out of his way for "his" daughter, an exceptional fact and the only example of its kind in the Gospels. At that time, losing a daughter was not an especially grave tragedy for a father. We must conclude therefore that there is a special, privileged relation between him and his "little daughter," to the exclusion of his wife. In the end, it is Jesus who reintroduces the couple and suggests only one thing to them: that they give something to eat to this young girl brought back to life.

That is why I think that the daughter was taught to live like a charming bird in a gilded cage, the powerless prisoner of her father and those about her, who did nothing to separate her from him.

Why do the Gospels show us the cure of the woman and the death of the little girl at one and the same moment?

The little girl is dying out of fear of causing her father to die. When a child or an adolescent or a son or a daughter accedes to his or her desire against the will of the parents, there is a scene, often accompanied by fits of anger, tears, cries. This is a fact of everyday life.

This represents the struggle of adolescents to live outside their family. They are said to be at the "age of ingratitude" . . . Ungrateful toward their parents, of course, who reproach them for it! It is not, alas, without guilt concerning their sexuality that young people negotiate this painful passage, and it is not without bitterness on the part of parents.

But when the child, who has a precise place in the pathology of a neurotic family—here the place is that of a doll, the privileged object of the father—wishes to abandon this place and live his or her own personal desire (providing that he or she still has the energy for it, which is rare after so many years of mutual parasitism), then the other sinks into neurasthenia and even suicide. Both are responses to despair, the former being its passive form and the latter its active. Jairus' daughter has given up the struggle for her life. The father is not aware that he is in large part responsible for this. He suffers, he is afraid, he calls on Jesus to help him.

And he gets the same responses as the woman with the hemorrhage (yet another detail in common in the two sto-

ries): "Do not be afraid; only have faith." "Your faith has restored you to health."

It is always a question of faith. To the woman Jesus says in effect, "You have always had what is necessary to have regular periods, but you did not know it. It is a man who can give you faith in yourself." Jesus was this man. In fact, a woman knows that she is feminine, feels that she is feminine, only through the eyes of a man who believes in her.

He says the same thing to Jairus: "Have faith in yourself, in your strength as a man and as a husband, and your daughter will live." In other words, "If you have faith in your strength as a husband, you will be able to say to your little girl, 'My little daughter, you are feminine, but not for me.'" And she will be able to live by and for another. Jesus is this other.

Why does he keep the crowd and all the people who were there weeping and wailing from witnessing the scene inside the house?

They are not bemoaning the little girl but rather the "star" that she represented, the spoiled daughter of the official of the synagogue. Had it been a question of the death of another little girl, would they have wept as many tears? But this was the daughter of a notable! The entire crowd was moved. A daughter whose father loved her so much—and what a father—this was something quite out of the ordinary!

Jesus does away with all the pathos, all the melodrama of the weeping and moaning, all the protections, all the customs that had shut up this little girl as an object, not a subject, for twelve years in the slumber of the heart. This

young girl was unaware of her desire to become an adult.
All she could do was dream of it as she appeared to sleep.

*"The child is not dead, but asleep," Jesus says. "But
they laughed at him." Why this scoffing? Do they take him
to be a charlatan?*

Yes, of course, but the laughter, the scoffing, is also a
resistance to an anxiety. When Thomas Edison presented
his phonograph to the Academy of Sciences, the academi-
cians all filed out of the room, saying scornfully: "Nobody's
going to take us for suckers duped by cheap sorcery!"

Whenever there is a disruption in the laws known up
until the time of the disruption, there is always someone
who is scornful, who denies that such a thing is possible.
This was the case for Pasteur, for Franklin, and so on.

Everything that is new provokes reaction, resistance.
Even today Freud arouses opposition and rejection. And
also Christ, even in our day . . . !

Newness, adventure, the unexpected, novelty, the
Good News—all arouse anxiety before they bring peace and
joy.

*And Jesus says, "Little girl, I tell you to get up." He
awakens her from this hypnosis that has paralyzed her.*

You are correct to speak of hypnosis, which does not
mean that she was not dead in the eyes of those around her.
But as far as death is concerned, and life as well, I repeat,
what is important is not what it *is* but what it *means*.

Here this child is numbed, frozen by a man who is not
yet castrated, not yet separated from his desire to be at once
a man and a woman; he has supplanted his wife, he has
lived through the love of his child. Father and daughter

were as one. When the latter began to have regular periods, became nubile, the father lost his blood. He began to suffer from a hemorrhage!

After this resurrection, Christ's first idea is to say to the parents, "Give her something to eat."

The parents have only to satisfy the physical needs of this child, not her desires. This child is dead, she has lost her appetite for living: she had been given everything without ever being able to desire anything by herself.

Now Christ has caused her to live as a healthy child who no longer belongs to her parents but to herself. "Give her something to eat; stop devouring her." Let her come to the freedom of her desire—and, of course, to its risks as well, since she is destined to leave her family soon.

They are stupefied . . .

They discover all of a sudden that the child that they loved is not the one who has come back to life. A resurrection is a rupture, a mutation. And here she is brought back to life. Instead of giving them this child to embrace, to cover with kisses, Jesus says to them: "Give her something to eat; that is your only role toward your daughter now."

"And say nothing about it; keep your mouths shut."

Let the life of this little girl who has been cured be itself the witness. No gossiping about her, no words that would make her the passive heroine of spectacular exploits. What is more, the parents might still boast about her and be vainglorious through her. They would all be objects of admiration. No, letting her eat and go on her way is a sufficient sign, in and of itself. It is she who must now take responsibility for her actions, who must speak in her own name.

At her "awakening," she has before her eyes her two parents, Jesus, and his disciples.

In obliging her mother to join her spouse at the moment of her awakening, Jesus initiates this girl into her future as a woman. He takes her by the hand, raises her up, and has her walk: he separates her from her father who is once again at his wife's side; he separates her, as once upon a time her mother was separated from her own father in order to marry.

Freed of her dependence on her father, Jairus' daughter awakens. The man Jesus offers her his hand and thus reveals to her her identity as a young girl. The mother is put back in her rightful place as a spouse. She can now be an example to her daughter, who, in preparing herself for the role as a woman, a wife, and a mother, will come to flower in love.

And what else does she see at the moment of her awakening? The society of men represented by Jesus' disciples. They welcome her through the chastity of their gaze and thus confirm her in her reborn femininity. Her childhood spent curled up in a ball is over.

In dying, she had only one father and now she discovers a happy couple, while at the side of the man who has given her back the joy of living, four chaste men greet her. It is almost like her enthronement in society.

A woman is thus recognized as a woman by a man. But who will aid a little girl to recognize herself as feminine?

A young girl recognizes herself as such through a chaste man and not through a possessive man. A little girl who has no value except through the possessive love of her father is not suited to enter the arena of the young women of society. I think that the role of the Apostles in this "psychodrama" is as important as that of the two parents who serve as witnesses.

In fact, when either fawned upon or scorned, a woman is alienated from her destiny to be someone who desires.

So here are two women who have different relations to men?

Yes, Jairus' daughter is not recognized as a subject, but is flattered as an object. The woman with the hemorrhage, also unrecognized, lonely, lost in the crowd, is the image of the needy woman abandoned by men. Both are excluded: the former is not yet introduced into society, and the latter is rejected by it.

Too adulated by men or too much ignored by them, a woman cannot know that she is a woman. She does not succeed in focusing her desire to be recognized as a woman by another or in giving living form to her femininity.

Today we would say that both of them were dying of psychosomatic illnesses, powerless as women, though as regards their age and their economic and social status they are diametrically opposed.

The dynamic of their feminine life is arrested.

The little girl, as I have said, is an object, a participant in her father's fame, the focus of the power fantasies for people of a society that adores her father's money and titles.

The woman with the hemorrhage is hurt by an imaginary castration.

On discovering the anatomical difference of the sexes and in the face of the pride of little boys, many little girls think that they are missing "something." Following this first disappointing setback, many young girls continue to have a very unflattering opinion of their sex, an intimate shame renewed each month after puberty by the period of sensed isolation imposed by the monthly menstrual flow, an isolation that is felt by the young girl to be a form of opprobrium. Because of their sex, many young girls also continue to have feelings of inferiority until the day that, through a man, they discover their value as a woman. What they thought of as a wound is revealed to them to be the prelude to love.

In this passage from the Gospel we discover, once again, human beings whose destiny has been prematurely arrested.

Yes, the source of their desire is exhausted because of a destructive emotional relation. They are both bound to their childhood bodies by a love tie that has not been broken.

Christ breaks this tie and makes them autonomous. Having been freed—the little girl from being overvalued, the woman from being scorned—they blossom—capable at last, after twelve years, the one of walking alone, the other of living as a woman.

The Raising
of Lazarus

The Gospel According to Saint John
Chapter XI, Verses 1 to 44

¹ There was a man named Lazarus who lived in the village
of Bethany with the two sisters, Mary and Martha, and he was
² ill.—•It was the same Mary, the sister of the sick man Lazarus,
who anointed the Lord with ointment and wiped his feet with
³ her hair. •The sisters sent this message to Jesus, "Lord, the
⁴ man you love is ill." •On receiving the message, Jesus said,
"The sickness will end not in death but in God's glory, and
through it the Son of God will be glorified."

⁵
⁶ Jesus loved Martha and her sister and Lazarus, •yet when
he heard that Lazarus was ill he stayed where he was for two
⁷ more days •before saying to the disciples, "Let us go to Ju-
⁸ daea." •The disciples said, "Rabbi, it is not long since the Jews
⁹ wanted to stone you; are you going back again?" •Jesus replied:

> "Are there not twelve hours in the day?
> A man can walk in the daytime without stumbling
> because he has the light of this world to see by;
> ¹⁰   but if he walks at night he stumbles,
> because there is no light to guide him."

¹¹ He said that and then added, "Our friend Lazarus is resting,
¹² I am going to wake him." •The disciples said to him, "Lord, if
¹³ he is able to rest he is sure to get better." •The phrase Jesus
used referred to the death of Lazarus, but they thought that by
¹⁴ "rest" he meant "sleep," so •Jesus put it plainly, "Lazarus is
¹⁵ dead; •and for your sake I am glad I was not there because
¹⁶ now you will believe. But let us go to him." •Then Thomas—

known as the Twin—said to the other disciples, "Let us go too, and die with him."

17 On arriving, Jesus found that Lazarus had been in the tomb
18 for four days already. •Bethany is only about two miles from
19 Jerusalem, •and many Jews had come to Martha and Mary to
20 sympathize with them over their brother. •When Martha heard that Jesus had come she went to meet him. Mary remained
21 sitting in the house. •Martha said to Jesus, "If you had been
22 here, my brother would not have died, •but I know that, even
23 now, whatever you ask of God, he will grant you." •"Your
24 brother," said Jesus to her, "will rise again." •Martha said, "I know he will rise again at the resurrection on the last day."
25 Jesus said:

"I am the resurrection.
If anyone believes in me, even though he dies he will live,
26 and whoever lives and believes in me
will never die.
Do you believe this?"

27 "Yes, Lord," she said, "I believe that you are the Christ, the Son of God, the one who was to come into this world."
28 When she had said this, she went and called her sister Mary, saying in a low voice, "The Master is here and wants to see
29 you." •Hearing this, Mary got up quickly and went to him.
30 Jesus had not yet come into the village; he was still at the
31 place where Martha had met him. •When the Jews who were in the house sympathizing with Mary saw her get up so quickly and go out, they followed her, thinking that she was going to the tomb to weep there.
32 Mary went to Jesus, and as soon as she saw him she threw
33 herself at his feet, saying, •"Lord, if you had been here, my brother would not have died." At the sight of her tears, and those of the Jews who followed her, Jesus said in great distress,
34 with a sigh that came straight from the heart, •"Where have
35 you put him?" They said, "Lord, come and see." •Jesus wept;
36 and the Jews said, "See how much he loved him!" •But there
37 were some who remarked, "He opened the eyes of the blind

38 man, could he not have prevented this man's death?" •Still
sighing, Jesus reached the tomb: it was a cave with a stone to
39 close the opening. •Jesus said, "Take the stone away." Martha
said to him, "Lord, by now he will smell; this is the fourth
40 day." •Jesus replied, "Have I not told you that if you believe
41 you will see the glory of God?" •So they took away the stone.
Then Jesus lifted up his eyes and said:

> "Father, I thank you for hearing my prayer.
42 > I knew indeed that you always hear me,
> but I speak
> for the sake of all these who stand around me,
> so that they may believe it was you who sent me."

43 When he had said this, he cried in a loud voice, "Lazarus,
44 here! Come out!" •The dead man came out, his feet and hands
bound with bands of stuff and a cloth around his face. Jesus
said to them, "Unbind him, let him go free."

Gérard Sévérin

We come now to the third resurrection, that of Lazarus. What strikes me in this story is the fact that Jesus makes people wait for him. Is this a caprice on his part?

Françoise Dolto

Christ has had an inkling of the possible failure of his mission, namely, that people would settle for a communion or a communication from body to body with him, even an imaginary one. Though necessary, perhaps, at a certain moment of his evolution and of the evolution of those around him, this communion now appears to him to be insufficient. It is necessary to go further.

The difference between the resurrection of Lazarus

and the two preceding resurrections is that Lazarus is a personal friend of Jesus'. This family in Bethany is dear to him, their home is a haven of repose for him. They call for his aid. Yes, his friend is ill, but is that a reason to interrupt his travels and change his present plans? As he knows, he has been forbidden to make Judaea his place of residence and must not put his own life in danger, not to mention the lives of his disciples, before his hour has come. This is not a caprice. He experiences a real personal trial and has no clear idea as to what he should do. I think that when he decides to go to Bethany it is because he knows then not only that Lazarus is dead but that it is the time in his mission to manifest the glory of God. He now has a message to transmit.

There are ordeals that are brought on by what psychoanalysis calls the "blocking mechanism." But there are also inevitable initiatory ordeals. This tragic week was necessary for Lazarus and his sisters and also necessary for Jesus so that he could see his mission clearly, above and beyond the personal wishes of his human heart. I think that is what he is referring to in his words about the hours of light and the hours of darkness.

In order to evolve, the human being must pass through suffering and mourning. There are certain painful experiences that are inevitable, that test the faith of human beings, but they pass with the night.

But why does he make them wait such a long time? When he arrives, Lazarus has been in the tomb for four days: "Lord, by now he will smell . . ." Why this delay?

Jesus himself explains: "Lazarus is dead; and for your sake I am glad I was not there because now you will believe."

This resurrection is a decisive turning point in Christ's life.

The problem that confronts Jesus is a twofold one: "My mission is not for people to live because I am present in the flesh or to die because I am no longer present in that way. It is faith in God and love for each other that must make them live."

It would mean possible failure if people loved him instead of believing in him, in his words, in his mission. That, it seems to me, is the first aspect of his problem.

The second aspect is a correlative one. He is the Way and the Life. He cannot hold people to him by his humanity, which would be a sort of deceptive seduction. He is a man, he has positive feelings, he therefore gives of his human love to other human beings. But he loves men in their development, not in any narcissistic interpersonal fixation.

His love is a love that evolves. He wishes himself to be a dynamic source of love stretching like a chain between human beings, his brothers and sisters in God. If his fleshly being served those who love him only as a mirror in which they found their own much-loved presence, his evolutionary mission to renew Judaism would be a failure.

The New Covenant that he came to reveal to men would not be sealed in their heart, the message he bore would be burdened by the flesh of his body, the mediator of the Word of Life through his acts and his words.

When he is absent his word must remain present, as much alive in the heart of those who have received it as though he were with them, sharing their daily life.

Lazarus' sisters reproach Christ for his abandonment of them, which they claim was the cause of their brother's death. This reproach is the touchstone of a "misunderstanding" in Lazarus' love (to assign its level) for Jesus, which was more for the person of Jesus than for his words.

So you believe that Lazarus was unable to bear the physical absence of Jesus?

Yes, he is no longer supported or sustained enough to continue to live. Martha says as much to Jesus: "If you had been here, my brother would not have died." A few moments later, it is Mary who says the same thing to Jesus: "Lord, if you had been here, my brother would not have died."

Since Christ had not answered the appeal addressed to him, Lazarus believed that he had been abandoned. He was no longer certain of Jesus' love for him and despaired of ever seeing him again. If he loved Lazarus, would not Jesus have been able to risk everything in the name of their friendship? (Lazarus knew very well that there were certain people in Judaea who wanted to stone Jesus to death.)

Is this a homosexual friendship?

Yes, on Lazarus' part it is more or less a passionate, narcissistic friendship. Lazarus despairs of being separated from Jesus, like a baby who is separated from its mother's breast and allows itself to die. Lazarus in fact needs Jesus. His love for Jesus is one of carnal dependence. If Jesus has forgotten him, as he believes, or if Jesus prefers his mission (or his safety), Lazarus no longer has faith in him or in his words.

And in what way did Jesus love Lazarus then?

His destiny is a heavy burden to live with; Jesus is tempted at certain moments to be a man like other men, to be a political leader, to be rich, to be powerful . . . and why not also to be loved for himself alone?[1] The devil is not the only tempter. Every human love must be tempting too.

Jesus of Nazareth is subject to what is human in himself just like the rest of us; he is subject to those modes of love-as-mirror to which all of us are conditioned from earliest childhood.

But then this is even clearer in the case of John. Is he not called "the disciple that Jesus loved"?

Yes, of course. John is what remains of Christ's narcissism, that is to say, the affective fixation on himself, the son of woman who, in the mirror of loving eyes, has become acquainted with himself, has become co-born, as each one of us loves his face when he looks into a mirror, or at least is not indifferent to that face.[2] John is like a mirror for Jesus. Like a mirror of his hidden life—before Cana—that was the preparation for the future. Perhaps Jesus renews his resources in this human being who is so much like him, the image of himself in his youth open to the future.

He gave John to the Virgin precisely because he was his alter ego, so as to replace himself as a social, human son and also so that Mary might love John and receive consolation for the death of her son Jesus.

John bore up under the death of Jesus because, in my opinion, he had to sustain Mary. For Mary, John was not a friend; he was another son.

[1] Matthew IV: 1–11; Luke IV: 1–13.
[2] "Co-born" is, once again, a pun in the original French. The phrase *a pris con-naissance* (has become acquainted) is, as the hyphen indicates, being employed here in its original compound sense of "birth" (*naissance*) and "with" (*co-*).

Thanks to this mission, John was able to bear up under his grief. For Jesus, John was the fleshly substitute for the son that death had stolen away from the mourning mother's chaste tenderness.

Lazarus, for his part, was fixated on Christ through the person of Jesus who was his light, but with Jesus absent, Lazarus walked in darkness. This is perhaps another interpretation of Jesus' words: "A man can walk in the daytime without stumbling . . . but if he walks at night he stumbles." Jesus was his sun, not Christ.

Hence Lazarus does not bear up under the trial of this separation from Jesus. He needs to be with Jesus Christ at regular intervals. Is that what he dies of—depression?

In my opinion, this is, in effect, an acute depression. He does not die through a fulfillment of his desire; rather, he dies from a lack, from a frustration of his desire for Jesus, from a lack of psychological and spiritual nourishment.

Lazarus still needed Jesus because he was not capable of being autonomous. Jesus is his nourishing father-mother. But it is precisely in this role, I repeat, that Jesus perceives, unequivocally, in the case of Lazarus the risk of failing in his mission if, in loving anyone, he hesitates in keeping his word and acting upon it.

Jesus risks failing in his mission because of one last remaining trace of narcissism: his presence in the flesh is powerful. It awakened Lazarus! This may be flattering for Jesus of Nazareth, but Christ cannot remain fixated on this self-indulgence, the baited trap of human narcissism present in each one of us.

What place does Christ have, then, for Lazarus? Is he his mirror, his auxiliary self?

Yes and no; it goes deeper than that. Jesus serves him as a placenta and as an umbilical cord.

Lazarus falls ill, he regresses to a vegetative state, because, with Christ absent, he can no longer draw his life from Jesus. Lacking the wherewithal to subsist without the presence of Jesus, he is like a tree cut off from its roots, like a fetus that is no longer nourished through the umbilical cord by a living placenta.

Lazarus sees in Jesus the person without whose presence he has no life. Jesus could live without Lazarus. Lazarus could not live without Jesus.

When a baby is born, the placenta ceases to live; it no longer serves any purpose. At the same time, the fetus can no longer live if the placenta is removed. Fetus that he is, Lazarus can no longer live without Jesus. Before meeting Jesus, his sisters were enough, but not afterward.

Lazarus is like a fetus that has died *in utero*. He is there, a human being who has returned to mother earth, wrapped in a shroud, with no more interpsychic communication with the living.

No longer drawing sap from the human person of Christ, the vegetative part of him now has nothing to live on. The death process, which causes every creature to undergo organic disorganization, reduces Lazarus' body to its earthly elements, by means of decomposition: the odor of putrid flesh comes forth from the tomb.

His body is now decomposing. Abandoned, Lazarus has lost the instinct for self-preservation. The one being in the world his life has depended on since he has learned to love is missing.

His mode of fixation on Jesus was as much a need of Jesus as it was a desire for fusion and narcissistic love. The ordeal of affective devitalization at this archaic level brought on the devitalization of the unconscious cohesive link between spirit and flesh. This destruction of this link is fatal to the body.

He dies, one might say, of an acute melancholic neurosis.

When Jesus meets Mary, Martha, and Lazarus and becomes their friend, Lazarus still has close ties to his two sisters. An unmarried adult male, he is attached to two women who are also unmarried. All three resemble inseparable children who have not been weaned in their parents' house. Or perhaps more like triplets who have not yet emerged into social life, each of them failing to take independent responsibility for his or her life through his or her own libido.

Notice also that these two sisters are fixated, like their brother, on the person of Christ. Martha is attached to him through works that stem from anal sublimation: she works with her hands, she organizes, she *does* things.

Mary is fixated on him in an adoration that is primarily oral: she sits at Jesus' feet and drinks the milk of his words, not moving, contemplating him. An affective situation revealing an oral transfer.

Of these two "girls," one of them, Martha, has worked, has bustled about on his behalf; the other, Mary, has drunk him in through her eyes and ears. As for the "boy," Lazarus, he died when Jesus was not there! A neurotic trio if there ever was one!

It may appear astonishing that Christ lends himself to these regressions or these unresolved fixations.

There is nothing unusual about this. Jesus can endorse and redeem all desires. He allows all human beings to live them, and then he transfigures them, but he does so through castration—that is to say, I repeat, by a separation, a rupture with the first being who has aroused their genuine desire. Beyond this mourning for their chosen object, he arouses in all humans this same desire to fulfill themselves in life, in relation to others.

Careful note should be taken of the fact that in the raising up of Lazarus, Christ also castrates himself. He separates himself from the remaining traces of carnality in the love that he experiences for this man and these women who adore him and whose home was a warm, welcoming one for him.

In another circumstance, as we have seen, he castrates the son of the widow of Nain: he offers him urethro-anal and genital castration. He weaned the daughter of Jairus from her father: oral castration; moreover, when this rupture has been successfully completed with respect to both her parents, it will include genital castration for the father if he is stripped of his desire for his daughter.

Jesus provides Lazarus with fetal castration, of which the umbilicus is the trace, as it is also the proof of mourning successfully completed with respect to the afterbirth, the amniotic sacs.

If there is a transference by Lazarus to Jesus, if Jesus represents both his father and his mother for the unconscious of Lazarus, you as a psychoanalyst must admit that Christ responded to this transference by a countertransference! This is dynamically inevitable within the libidinal system.

Of course; that is obvious. Not only does Jesus accept Lazarus' friendship, which does him good; he also gives him his friendship in return. Is he not told, "Lord, the man you love is ill"?

We must go further still. This countertransference is a response of Jesus' unconscious to Lazarus' unconscious.

In the face of Lazarus' death, Christ shudders, weeps, he is moved, troubled, trembling, shaking, as though contaminated by the cold of death. A tree in a cyclone.

His unconscious shares some part of the death of Lazarus. In order to be able to free Lazarus from his infantile fixation on him, in order to separate Lazarus from the placenta that Jesus represents, Jesus is obliged to relive in himself what there is of a human fixation (and a countertransferred one on Lazarus). He must regress in his own history, return there where Lazarus is. Jesus must free himself of his placenta. He is obliged to relive his separation as a child who was rooted in the human uterus. He groans and he weeps.

You must understand that the two changes, one undergone by Lazarus, one by Jesus, are parallel. It is necessary for Jesus to suffer what Lazarus suffered in order to understand the traces of narcissism remaining in him that link him to his friends in everyday life. He discovers how much he still needed his friends, and in a groan of love he separates himself from them.

Christ felt at this point that he could be trapped by the projections of people on him, and at the same time he felt that he could be trapped by his own projections on those around him.

That is true. Christ detaches himself from those traces of passionate love remaining in him as a human brother to men. Jesus renounces himself. By detaching himself from Lazarus, another self of his, he brings Lazarus back to life, he awakens him, he makes him exist. In a certain way, Christ becomes the placenta that is abandoned, the remains of a fetus that had become a newborn nursing baby wrapped in swaddling clothes.

Attuned to Lazarus, Jesus separates himself from this confusion that a man who had encountered God only in another man would have, a man who would confuse his desire for the spiritual with his mingled desire and love for a spiritual man. In Lazarus' case, this confusion has distorted his desire for God.

As though there were a confusion between the Gospel and the one who presents the Gospels.

At this moment, Jesus, the Son of Man, frees himself from the confusion between our desire for the spiritual and our instinct of self-preservation.

As long as we live, life appears sacred to us, but the desire to survive can make us forget that true life is not of this world. Beyond the conditioning of time and space that affects our life as beings of flesh and emotions, the spirit that animates us is called, from our conception to our death, throughout our lives, to a fulfillment elsewhere.

In the wilderness, the devil does not deserve to be loved, but the objects that he offers would tempt any man. Jesus emerges victorious over this temptation.

On the other hand, Lazarus and his sisters seem most agreeable to him. In their home he can rest in a very human fashion. His mission was making progress. He had to separate himself from this last haven of repose, of the sort that can be a temptation for every man of action.

The way in which Christ carries out this separation, which changes everything for him just as it gives Lazarus a new life, is truly heroic and prefigures the supreme separation of his Passion.

With the resurrection of Lazarus, Jesus definitely becomes an object of scandal for the Jews. From this moment on, they seek a way and a time to kill him.

Lazarus emerges from the tomb. The Gospel makes no mention of any look exchanged, any thanks offered to Jesus by Lazarus or his sisters.

At that point Jesus, the man, is now prepared to die.

Chapter VII

THE
OINTMENT
OF
BETHANY

45 Many of the Jews who had come to visit Mary and had seen
46 what he did believed in him, ·but some of them went to tell the
47 Pharisees what Jesus had done. ·Then the chief priests and
Pharisees called a meeting. "Here is this man working all these
48 signs," they said, "and what action are we taking? ·If we let
him go on in this way everybody will believe in him, and the
Romans will come and destroy the Holy Place and our na-
49 tion." ·One of them, Caiaphas, the high priest that year, said,
50 "You don't seem to have grasped the situation at all; ·you fail
to see that it is better for one man to die for the people, than
51 for the whole nation to be destroyed." ·He did not speak in
his own person, it was as high priest that he made this proph-
52 ecy that Jesus was to die for the nation—·and not for the nation
only, but to gather together in unity the scattered children
53 of God. ·From that day they were determined to kill him.

Chapter XII, Verses 1 to 8

1 Six days before the Passover, Jesus went to Bethany, where
2 Lazarus was, whom he had raised from the dead. ·They gave
a dinner for him there; Martha waited on them and Lazarus
3 was among those at table. ·Mary brought in a pound of very
costly ointment, pure nard, and with it anointed the feet of
Jesus, wiping them with her hair; the house was full of the
4 scent of the ointment. ·Then Judas Iscariot—one of his dis-
5 ciples, the man who was to betray him—said, ·"Why wasn't
this ointment sold for three hundred denarii, and the money
6 given to the poor?" ·He said this, not because he cared about
the poor, but because he was a thief; he was in charge of the
common fund and used to help himself to the contributions.
7 So Jesus said, "Leave her alone; she had to keep this scent for
8 the day of my burial. ·You have the poor with you always, you
will not always have me."

Gérard Séverin

*In emerging from the tomb, you say, Lazarus does not
turn toward Jesus, expresses no gratitude toward him. Lazarus is therefore presumably autonomous now, and Jesus is
left on his own by him . . .*

*But doesn't the rest of the story demonstrate the con-
trary? In this passage of the Gospels, we see Jesus at his
friend's side; they sup together. And hasn't Lazarus returned to his sisters?*

Françoise Dolto

When Lazarus emerges from the tomb, Jesus says:
"Let him go free." Lazarus is changed, mutated. I repeat:
Lazarus does not seek Jesus out, he leaves with his grave-
clothes. It is Jesus who says, "Unbind him, let him go free."
Lazarus has the right to be autonomous and now has the
desire and the power to be so as well.

Previously, he was a man only if the man Jesus was
there to tell him so, to be the guarantor of the fact that he
was a man. Once he has emerged from the fetal life of the
tomb, Lazarus no longer needs the man Jesus in order to
exist: the words of Christ, pronounced in a loud voice—
"Lazarus, here! Come out!"—makes him become a man and
frees him of his dependence on Jesus. From now on, he can
love Jesus in an adult fashion.

In fact, one might expect that, as he comes to life
again, Lazarus would go to this being who awaits him, as a
nursing baby goes into the waiting arms of his mother. Jesus
causes Lazarus to emerge from his fetal state. From now on
Lazarus no longer needs to be carried by anyone.

He now lacks nothing; he has everything he needs to

be a free man in society. Jesus has said: "Unbind him, let him go free."

When you say "Jesus is now prepared to die," does that mean that he is completely denarcissised and hence depressive, that he feels alone, good for nothing except to die?

One cannot live without narcissism. I say that here, in this heroic resurrection, Jesus has detached himself from that ancient human narcissism and transfers it to the Word of God rather than retaining it in his being of flesh. It is sublimated into his mission. There remains nothing that binds him to his past.

When Jesus and Lazarus meet for this meal at Bethany, they are both changed. Lazarus is a man. Jesus is now totally engaged in his Father's business.

But why is it that people want to kill Jesus immediately following this resurrection?

He is no longer a human being like the others. He is a disturbing figure on the margins of society.

But there have been other resurrections before this one. Why is it that they conspire to kill him only after the resurrection of Lazarus?

It is because of the more profound "meaning" of this resurrection, because of the publicity that has grown up about it, and the resulting fear of people in authority that their "clientele" may leave them. "If we let him go in this way, everybody will believe in him, and the Romans will come and destroy the Holy Place and our nation."

Jesus frightens people; he is experienced as a threat—he overturns what holds this society together: the rites, the Temple, the high priests, and so on, and by that very fact he destroys the ritual guilt, the debt of the body to God.

When someone magnifies desire to this point, there is no more room for a sense of guilt. It is total freedom. How keep united a society of people who would be entirely free, who would no longer obey the high priests?

By organizing itself institutionally, Christianity began once more to make "Jews"—it created believers on an assembly line, who were alienated from other living persons and who supposedly represented the symbolic Phallus, the Impossible, Otherness, Elsewhere . . .

But is it possible for a society to exist without the alienation of desire?

If it is a society with a hierarchy, it is impossible. When the life of a society is based on exchanges between peers, it is possible.

But is it possible for a society to exist without a hierarchy?

Until now, that has not been possible because of "intertransferences," the need to seek values based on power and authority arbitrarily attributed to certain people who are more "initiated" than oneself. When we were small we sought parents who had power over us and who knew everything; in obedience to them, in our dependence on them, we felt a sense of security.

In fact, I do not know if it is possible for a religion to implant itself in a society without a hierarchy and above all without a combination of phallic values and impulses: initiator-initiated, decision-submission, and so on, all related to rules and rites that involve guilt feelings if there are failures in their observation.

This dross, inherent in social life and in political security, is foreign to the Gospel.

Let us go back to this meal in Bethany. Lazarus is "among those at table." But in this story, what is most astonishing is what happens between Mary, the sister of Lazarus, and Jesus.

Mary "wastes" a very expensive ointment that costs three hundred denarii, the annual salary of a worker of this period! What luxury! On another occasion Jesus counsels the rich young man to leave his wealth behind, but from Mary he accepts magnificent ostentation and luxury.

It is up to each of us to know, in his own life, what is a luxury and what a necessity, to know what to keep and what to let go of.

But Mary here shows something of the change that has taken place in her since the resurrection of her brother. She, who was once merely passive at the feet of Jesus, is now active. Jesus has rearoused in Mary the dynamic of desire, which goes farther than passivity. She has now become a woman who is not simply passive; she can act for a man, she gives everything she is capable of giving. She gives pleasure. She who "drank him in" with her eyes and her ears now anoints his feet with an ointment of great price.

But what is the relation between Mary and Jesus in the course of this supper?

It is a demonstration of a wild and active love of

Christ, but all those present may also enjoy the ointment poured out.

There are two stories about ointment poured out on Christ. This one in the Gospel of John and one in the Gospel of Luke (VII: 36–50).

That fact is not without interest, for we thus discover that there are two women presented in the Gospels. In John, Mary is the sister of Lazarus. In Luke, Mary is not the sister of Lazarus, but a woman of easy virtue.

Before this, in their mode of loving, these two women "took" only. Now they give, and give in public where all can see and know of it; they declare their love through their gesture.

The Gospels have preserved the stories of these two examples of women who loved Jesus and manifested their love in the same way. When a woman loves a man, she gives herself, forgets herself, forgets whether she is an upright woman or a prostitute. Aren't these two types of women present in every woman who loves a man?

These two women thus express their love. Jesus accepts the homage of their feeling as women who give and who, out of love, risk the criticism of others.

But why does he say of the sister of Lazarus: "Leave her alone; she had to keep this scent for the day of my burial"?

It is precisely by these words that Jesus brings about a rupture between himself and Mary. She eroticizes her homage, and Jesus replies that he is elsewhere.

Perhaps without realizing it herself, Mary reveals his approaching death to him. Death arouses in every man the future horror of the stinking putrefaction of his body. Did not Martha say of Lazarus in Mary's hearing, "Lord, by now he will smell"? Between Mary and Jesus there is perhaps a common premonition of his death. Lazarus and his death are still implicitly present. A moment of change, both for Mary and for Christ.

Just as Mary, his mother, had revealed to him in Cana that his public life had begun, it may be that Mary of Bethany revealed to him with her ointment, through her love and her intuition, that the hour of his death was at hand.

Chapter VIII

THE PARABLE
OF
THE SAMARITAN

The Gospel According to Saint Luke
Chapter X, Verses 25 to 37

25   There was a lawyer who, to disconcert him, stood up and said to him, "Master, what must I do to inherit eternal life?"
26   He said to him, "What is written in the Law? What do you
27   read there?" •He replied, "You must love the Lord your God with all your heart, with all your soul, with all your strength,
28   and with all your mind, and your neighbor as yourself." •"You have answered right," said Jesus, "do this and life is yours."
29   But the man was anxious to justify himself and said to Jesus,
30   "And who is my neighbor?" •Jesus replied, "A man was once on his way down from Jerusalem to Jericho and fell into the hands of brigands; they took all he had, beat him and then
31   made off, leaving him half dead. •Now a priest happened to be traveling down the same road, but when he saw the man, he
32   passed by on the other side. •In the same way a Levite who came to the place saw him, and passed by on the other side.
33   But a Samaritan traveler who came upon him was moved with
34   compassion when he saw him. •He went up and bandaged his wounds, pouring oil and wine on them. He then lifted him on to his own mount, carried him to the inn and looked after him.
35   Next day, he took out two denarii and handed them to the innkeeper. 'Look after him,' he said, 'and on my way back I
36   will make good any extra expense you have.' •Which of these three, do you think, proved himself a neighbor to the man who
37   fell into the brigands' hands?" •"The one who took pity on him," he replied. Jesus said to him, "Go, and do the same yourself."

Françoise Dolto

This is a parable that has made a great impression on me! I heard it during vacation when I was a child . . . I listened to it in amazement. Then the priest climbed into the pulpit for his sermon. His preaching went something like this: "My dearly beloved brothers, Jesus asks us to love our neighbor, to pay heed to all sorts of troubles, to give of our time and our life to those less fortunate than ourselves. Let us not be selfish, like this priest and this Levite who see and yet pass by."

Gérard Séverin

And you did not agree with this explanation?

This parish priest said precisely the opposite of what I had just heard from the Gospel text. He massacred this parable!

First of all, Christ blames neither the priest nor the Levite. He simply recounts facts. He does not pass judgment. Let us do likewise!

Jesus answers two questions; first, What must one do to have one's "name inscribed in heaven?" and secondly, Who is my neighbor?

Jesus answers by recounting a parable. On the road from Jerusalem to Jericho a man is attacked by a band of thieves. He is stripped and left half-dead. A priest comes by, and then a Levite, both of them men of God in the eyes of the Jews. They see him but prudently go their way.

A Samaritan comes by on his travels. He is all alone, sitting on his mount, whistling perhaps. Since in the next few minutes he is going to set the dying man on "his own mount," it may be that he is a merchant who is leading along a donkey or a mule to bear his goods while he rides on a second one. I am inventing perhaps, but that is the way I see things.

He is a Samaritan . . . He is not a leftist intellectual of his day. He is not a "pillar of the synagogue." He is one of those people who do not have much to boast of: no church, few virtues. They are very close to nature, they are not "spiritual" men. He is the way he is!

He sees that abandoned man on the edge of the road. He draws closer. He has seen him because he had a mind on the alert: like every traveler of the period, he knew that he risked being attacked by bandits. In this man lying wounded on the edge of the road, he recognizes himself. He might have been that man. He will perhaps suffer the same fate on his next trip.

So the priest and the Levite were unable to recognize themselves in this man who has been beaten?

Of course not. No one attacked these men of God to strip them of their belongings.

And doubtless this Samaritan had a little time and also the strength of character that made him approach this man who has been so cruelly dealt with. He cares for him with the means he has at hand: he sterilizes his wounds with wine and soothes them with oil. He sets him on his mount in order to leave him at the first inn he comes to, where he too, doubtless, spends the night. The next day he leaves the inn-keeper a little money, saying that he will pass by there on his way back and reimburse him for any expenditures on behalf of the man.

He has seen, he has helped, he has put this man, wounded by life, in good hands, and he continues on his way. He takes care of his own personal affairs now. He goes away. Jesus does not even tell us that he greets the man whose life he has saved!

He has "lost" or "given" a little of his time by setting

this man on his own mount, which means symbolically that he takes charge of his bodily needs: he carries him, he mothers him. He also treats him as a father would, since he provides the money to get the wounded man back on his feet again.

Jesus asks in essence: "Which of these three men acted like the neighbor of this dehumanized man, reduced to corporeal and social powerlessness and who, if he were left in the state in which he was, would die without a word?"

The lawyer answers: "The one who took pity on him." "Go, and do the same yourself," Jesus adds.

That is to say, one must have pity, devote oneself to and take care of others, as this Samaritan has done and as your parish priest said to do earlier!

Christ here says nothing about that.

Who is the neighbor? For this poor man who has been robbed, beaten, stripped naked, it is the Samaritan. It is the Samaritan who has behaved like his neighbor. Christ thus demands that the man lying half-dead along the roadside love this Samaritan who has saved his life and to love him as he loves himself.

It is to the one who has been saved that Jesus teaches love. All his life he is to love the man from whom he has received attention, assistance, and material aid, the one without whom he would be dead. He is never to forget this man who has put him back in the saddle.

In the final analysis, then, Christ demands that we always recognize a debt toward our fellow, toward the Samaritans of our life?

According to Christ, all our life long we must recognize a debt toward the person who has shouldered our burdens at a time we could not have continued on our way alone. Whether we recognize it or not, we are indebted to the person who helps us in our moments of distress.

Thus we find ourselves debtors for eternity, dependent slaves—let us admit it—slaves of him who has been of some usefulness to us.

No, neither slaves nor dependent but rather loving freely out of gratitude. The Samaritan model from this Gospel leaves the other man free. He departs from our path and continues along his own. We can repay the debt of love and thankfulness we bear toward the known or unknown person who has helped us only by doing the same for others.

So others to whom we do good, whom we help out, will help us pay a debt and allow us to have a clear conscience!

When you are a "Samaritan," Christ says, you must ignore both the debt and the gratitude.

Unselfishness means forgetting one's generous gesture. The unselfish person doesn't have to banish the memory of it; that's already done.

It is an act of genital sublimation. It is like the mother who gives birth to a child. It is an act of love—it is something given. As in a loving coitus, it is something given.

But who will remember? The child. He owes a life and remains obliged to do the same thing himself for his own children or his life's companions. But not out of "duty" or out of "justice." It is a current of love. If it is blocked, it means death.

How many times we hear of people who are convinced that they have been charitable or generous and who later reproach others for lacking gratitude: "When I think of all the sacrifices that I've made for you . . . and now you're leaving me . . . you're going to another country . . . you're marrying a girl I don't care for . . ." or "When I think of everything I've done for this man, and now he is abandoning me."

It is not to the "Samaritan" that gratitude should be shown. We are to think of what he has done for us and act likewise toward another.

If he who has been "charitable" harbors within himself some sort of demand toward the one whom he has helped, if he expects gratitude, he proves that he was really seeking to buy someone and was not in fact a "Samaritan" at all.

But who is our neighbor in this day and age?

Our neighbor is everyone who, as destiny would have it, has happened to be there when we needed aid and has given it to us without our having asked for it, and who has helped us without even remembering it. Such persons have given to us from their abundance. They have taken us in hand for a time, in a place where their destiny crossed our path.

Our neighbor is the "thou" without whom there would be no "I" within us, in a moment when, deprived of physical or moral resources, we could no longer be a father or a mother to ourselves, when we could no longer help ourselves or guide ourselves.

All those who, like brothers and in an unselfish way, have taken responsibility for us until we were able to gather our strength once again and then have left us free to go on our way—every one of these have been our "neighbor."

Hence our neighbor is the man not of good words, but the man whose help is effective in moments of distress. It is the simple, "material" man. Is it the anonymous man moved by pity who has saved us from disaster?

Yes. Christ, who recounts this parable to teach us who our neighbor is, indicates to us that this neighbor gives us support at the moment when our loneliness, our unconscious distress, our unconscious destitution would have made us powerless to survive without him.

The "neighbor," the "Samaritan," is a man, you say, who may be considered today to be someone who shows himself to be our neighbor through the intermediary of a group, a labor union, a party, a Catholic aid society, a consumer group, a parent-teacher association, an organization of marriage counselors, Amnesty International . . .

Quite so.

It is more difficult today to live this "adventure" of the Samaritan: there are the police to take care of bandits, there are first-aid units to take care of the injured. Many organized groups have taken over the task of rendering aid: doctors, psychologists, lawyers, politicians, and so on, and they make me useless, unresponsible for what happens to my fellow . . . and to me. I no longer have any reason to concern myself with those in society who lie helpless; there are people who are paid to do that.

It is true, in this era of ours, that when someone who is hurt is lying along the roadside, there is a first-aid unit called "Police-Secours" [here in France]. But there is always a place for helping others, though it is becoming more dangerous now.

In fact, he who gives aid takes serious risks! He will have to prove that he did not cause the accident. It will demand his time, strength, and even more than that: in fact, the person who is hurt, recognizing in him the first person that he has seen, may affirm, in all good faith, that his savior is his assailant.

Law requires that someone be responsible. We tend to think that if someone takes care of a person who is hurt, it is because he is involved in some way. It is a highly ambiguous state of affairs.

The same is true in the case of hitchhikers; one is responsible for them if one picks them up!

Humans have made laws that run counter to our charitable impulses. They make charity a source of guilt.

Would you agree that there ought to be fewer institutions, fewer paid organizations?

No. I believe that the Christian religion, through its mystique, has permitted the creation of laws of assistance. This social organization was born of a feeling of charity, but nowadays all the employees of these institutions are paid, their work has become anonymous, and the warmth manifest in the relationship between the Samaritan and the man who was robbed has generally disappeared from the relationship between the representative of the organized group and the one who is assisted.

So it is important, then, to be moved with compassion, as the Samaritan is?

It is this emotion of compassion which is the basis of

interpsychic communication between men. There is physical assistance, which requires competence and is paid for, and then there is the emotion of compassion, which makes us human. When the latter is lacking, it is because service has been institutionalized or because the encounter is not unique, not unexpected as in the parable, but rather a habit, a "breadwinning" proposition or an exciting profession. The person assisted becomes merely an object. There is no longer a human relation.

Let us return to the text of the parable.

Once the man found lying half-dead along the roadside has been placed in the hands of the innkeeper, the Samaritan pays for his care. He promises to return by way of the inn, to pay any additional costs if this is necessary. Is this a friendship aborning?

Not at all. I see this Samaritan, as I have said, as a man of action with a positive bent. He has seen the battered man as another self and has aided him materially. But though he has helped him, he will not love this man for the rest of his life. After he has gone a mile or so, he will have forgotten this man entirely. He will doubtless think of him on his return when he pays the additional bill, ask for news of him, but then completely forget him.

But the one who has been helped, for his part, must never forget his savior, whether he is known or unknown to him. This is a commandment that is just as important as the one to love God with all one's heart, with all one's being.

So this parable presents us with a different point of view regarding people's relations to each other: thankfulness, gratitude toward strangers.

There is more to it than that. It seems to me that this parable sheds a twofold light on our way of living.

—First of all, it reveals our lifelong love for any person who has saved us when we were deprived of everything, in a state of distress, abandoned by one and all, including ourselves. That is what is new in the parable.

—Secondly, it offers an example of conduct, of a way of acting. When, like this Samaritan, you have a little time and the material capability, do not turn your back on someone whom you see to be in trouble.

When you are not occupied in doing something else and have a surplus of energy, give to the person along your way who is in need, if you can. But do not do anything more. Do not let yourself be distracted from your work. Do not be deflected from your way.

• Do not be held back by the one whom you have saved.

• Do not be bound by the gratitude you feel to the person who has helped you, but rather, do as he does.

• Do not be stopped by the memory of the person whom you have been able to help. Remember that you owe your survival to another; love this other in your heart, and when the occasion presents itself, do unto another as he has done unto you.

This stranger, this Samaritan, has acted like a brother to anonymous humanity, without thought of origin, race, religion, or class. Let the person who owes him his new strength and his return to the human community, do likewise.

That, it seems to me, is the charity that Christ wanted to bring about in his New Covenant.

Christ nonetheless puts this Samaritan before us as an

example: we must take care of others, give of our life, of our time, for those less fortunate than ourselves, as your parish priest put it!

The point of the parable is to love whoever has been close to us while we were on this earth. This is not giving our life, our time, but rather, it is helping a human being without that act hindering our activities in any way. Nothing to lose, nothing to gain. And if someone some day has helped us recover from a sorrow, a depression, let us remember it all our life long.

A moment ago you were speaking of caring for others "in an unselfish way." Do you as a psychoanalyst believe that forgetfulness of self, gratuitous giving, detachment exist?

Unselfishness does not exist in the human being. Even in parents' love one does not encounter the gift that is absolutely free: they care for their children only in order that they, the parents, may not die. Children are the sign for them of living beyond their own death. Loving one's children is fighting against one's death.

Children can leave the family home, no longer love their parents . . . What counts is that having profited so greatly from the example that has been given them, these children, once they have become parents, love their children in turn, even if, in their turn, these children are ungrateful to them.

The Bible nowhere enjoins children to love their parents. They are told to honor them,[1] to give them the wherewithal to live in the destitution of their old age.

[1] Exodus XX: 12; Mark VII: 10.

It is fine if there are interhuman relations between parents and children as between other beings with whom one has affinities. But they are nowhere enjoined to love their parents.

One loves one's neighbors, but there are parents who are not their children's neighbors.

You touch a sensitive nerve here. One is so much in the habit of imagining that the love of parents is generous, beneficent . . .

The absolutely free gift does not exist . . . except for certain pious or militant souls who deceive themselves.

Eating and drinking bring on defecating and urinating. That is the law. One always takes—and one always pays!

There is always an exchange. There is always something that is taken in return for what is exchanged.

One can in fact doubt the unselfishness of the Samaritan. He identifies with the man who was beaten and stripped of his belongings—but seeing oneself as a tattered object is not unselfish.

This is always the way in which one enters into contact with the other: one encounters oneself in the person of the other, who becomes our mirror. It is to oneself, narcissistically projected, that one brings aid. And that is what goes by the name of unselfishness.

But there do exist parents who save their child at the price of their own lives.

Of course, morally healthy parents, like animals who nourish their young, would go through fire to save their little ones. This is the law of life of mammals, and we are mammals too. And people who are not vicious give this assistance when it is a question of their own children. They save them as best they can from the greatest visible danger and hand them over as soon as possible to the doctor or the educator who is more expert than they.

But even then there is projection: to give one's life for one's child is to realize one's ideal of what a mother should be! In saving my child, I also save myself as a mother.

But in order to project ourselves into another, we must see him or imagine him to be like us in some way. But it is not a question of confusing oneself with the other: he has his own identity. This identifying with another is therefore not totally unselfish, because one projects himself and because it is partially to oneself that one does good in the other. It is in this sense that the Samaritan is "moved with compassion" for the other . . . for himself.

But Christ does not tell us to do good in the other; he does not tell us to use the other to live ourselves! Christ says that it is he himself that one finds in the other—"in so far as you neglected to do this to one of the least of these, you neglected to do it to me." It is not ourselves we find!

It is he! He does not forbid us identification since he says to us to "love . . . your neighbor as yourself." But how can we love each other when so often we hate ourselves and project what we hate onto others? That is doubtless what the priest and the Levite do.

It is because Christ loves us that we can love ourselves: through his teaching he heals the memory we have of not being entirely loved by our parents.

If we do not engage in generous acts because we lack parental example or because we have not understood this projection of our love onto someone else, Jesus wants us to realize that he is the recipient of the love we show to those less fortunate than ourselves. He thus restores those whose parents lived badly, loved badly, and were unable or did not know how to raise them; all the parents did was project themselves onto their children while not being able to recognize in them free persons.

But then, according to you, if the Levite and the priest had supposed that this man left half-dead was either another Levite or a son of a priest of the synagogue, they would not have turned away from the dying man.

They would have hastened to lend him aid. But then, in fact, to whom would they have lent their aid? To one of their own kind, to someone like them, with the same status and certain values in common. They would have cared for a privileged victim, a man of their rank. Identification and projection would have been possible.

Christ chose to cite the Samaritan as an example because he was a man without status, a stranger, a heretic. His reputation is in little danger if he associates with a nobody! Free of the fear of gossip, he does not stop to consider the qualities of the wounded man but only the fact that he is a human being, one of our species, an anonymous stranger.

This is an example of someone who is not hampered by principles or by self-complacency, someone who does not think beyond the end of his nose, who does what he does naturally.

I emphasize, by the way, this strength that has its origins in the detachment from his own reputation, something that is natural to this Samaritan and difficult to attain for most human beings.

In the end Christ tells us to care for others to the de-

gree that this aid does not perturb us in any way, does not make us leave our place or set aside our obligations. If one forces himself, he ends up being destroyed or parading his virtues, is that right?

Not "to the degree that" . . . ! This Samaritan did not go a single inch out of his way; his naïveté acts without a secret philosophy or a secret good conscience. There is a situation, and he approaches it artlessly, spontaneously.

Christ teaches us to be "natural," too—sincere, free of excessive zeal for doing the right thing, unself-conscious about our charity—just like the Samaritan whose detachment emphasizes his permanent openness to others. No alarums or excursions! He does not overdo things—in fact, he just falls short of being stingy. He does only what is strictly necessary. He acts in an efficient way.

Along those same lines, Christ blames neither the priest nor the Levite who turned away.

If they step aside and go their own way, if they avoid getting too close to this man they have observed, it is perhaps because they didn't have the necessary time or attention at their disposal. Perhaps it is also proof of a great weakness in their personalities: that they were in fact incapable of rendering service to a wounded man. They did what they had to do according to the place that was theirs. Jesus neither blames nor stigmatizes them.

One must know how to test himself. If we are incapable of rendering service, let us be realistic enough not to do it; we would only do it badly.

If we become free enough and strong enough, then we can help, without turning aside from our own path.

The important thing here is that after his act, the Samaritan goes on his way with his virtues in no way diminished and in no way enhanced.

So there is neither self-interest nor generosity in this story, and the Samaritan merely acts in accordance with the nature of things?

In this sense, one could continue this parable in an amusing way by saying: "Of course, this Samaritan is a merchant, and it is a future client that he is putting back on his feet! Of what use is a man stripped naked, perhaps an outlaw, to the priest and the Levite? They will not sell him clothes some day . . . And he will not shed light on the Scriptures for them."

Neither the unselfishness nor the "charitable virtue" that one would like to see in it really exist in this story.

One can imagine—why not?—a meeting in the market between the Samaritan merchant and his recovered protégé: "Ah, is that really you, the man who was lying along the roadside? Well then, what are you going to buy from me today?" That is to say, he really contributed to the recovery of a human being for the sake of commerce, never departing from his own commitment to business.

Christ sets him up as an example for us because he is a man who lives on the plane of material exchanges and who, thanks to this fact, is also capable of considering the human body, as such—independent of its status or recognized social or moral value or of its race—to be worth something in the world of economics.

It is all part of a way of seeing human life as a series of relationships, in which every relationship, regardless of how material it may be, reflects another relationship, another alliance announced by Jesus—that of charity coexistent and present, however invisibly, in every honest human encounter—that is, when a free man behaves toward another so as to make him still more free.

True love creates no dependence, no allegiance.

It is a business transaction—a give and take?

It is a transaction between physical persons from which there is no material gain. It seems to be a gift, but in fact it is a business transaction.

It is therefore a transaction, or rather a trade—I give to you, you give to me—but something else suddenly springs forth from this exchange?

I have given you something and you have given me nothing back. I have in no way profited or benefited. But you have had the benefit of knowing that you are loved, that you have been loved, and that you love. From this there arises a new link of a new covenant, an "alliance": a love that brings no commercial benefit or profit.

The Samaritan gave without receiving anything in return, and the badly injured man can do the same with others.

"Go and do the same yourself," Jesus says. "Love . . . your neighbor as yourself," that is to say, "Never forget this surplus value of vitality that your neighbor has given you as a gift, without impoverishing himself. In passing, he has permitted you to stand up and go on your way."

The fulfillment of self through a superabundance that has overflowed from the neighbor and shed its light and influence upon the destitute—that is the essence of all interaction. This holds true even if the neighbor, as we said, has projected himself into the destitute individual, because our psychic makeup does not allow us to encounter the other in any other way.

Radiating without impoverishing oneself is the gift that belongs only to those whose hearts are free and open.

It is also a metaphor, in adult life, of the pure and helpful love of parents for their little children while they remain physically helpless.

You will agree that many parents sacrifice for their children and that their life as parents is not easy. How many parents, how many, have had to toil long and hard to improve the well-being of someone else?

If they are true parents they act in this way without parading their virtues, without even feeling that they are making a sacrifice: they are really incapable of acting otherwise!

Their attitude would be a perverted one if, having accomplished their desire as parents, they demanded of their children that they be grateful. Parents set the example for their children who have become parents to behave in the same way toward their children.

To sum up, couldn't one say that in the encounters we have, our center is in the other? The more the other is our heart, the more even our exchange will be?

One could also say: "Our soul is the other." Taken individually, each one of us can know nothing of his or her soul. We will never know if we have a soul. The soul that we are vaguely aware of—the vibrant, ultimate focal point of our supposed identity—in short, the soul that we "have" is in the other. Otherwise there would not even be such things as words or communication.

If "I" and its mysterious participation in the being to which "I" lay claim had not come from another—father, mother, to begin with, and then companions along life's way—"I" would no longer participate in being.

You mean that if "I" am immured within myself, if "I" attempt to coincide only with myself, "I" lose being, "I" wither away in self-conceit?

Everyone wishes to save his little soul, the little something that he has, whereas what we really have is the other. "He who saves his soul shall lose it," Christ has said, "and he who loses it shall save it."

So why speak of a soul to save? These are words that are nonsense, words that are foreign to the message of the New Covenant and foreign to the most elementary psychology.

This mania for saving one's soul corresponded to a moment in the history of the Church when it was condemned, we might say, by the philosophy of an era, the philosophy wherein the philosopher said: "I think, therefore I am." Another stupid and dead utterance!

In fact, I cannot think except with the words of another. In time and space there is the encounter between a living being and words received from others that he assembles and repeats for himself. But from whom has he taken his existence, from whom has he learned to live? In the face of whom does he say "I"? Where is this "I" who thinks?

What should have been said was: "There is something that thinks and I express it." If I know you as a listening creature, I know myself as a speaking creature. Without you I have no existence. But existence is not the whole of being, existence is merely a perceptible phenomenon of being.

Isn't the existence of a man the shadow of Being? And isn't what we call our "soul" our luminous and invisible identifying fetish?

All this amounts to saying that the other who recognizes us as a brother of humanity is our humanizing mirror.

He can return us to our life's journey of going forward and becoming. That is what this beautiful story of the Samaritan tells us!

He is free of intellectual, moral, or social prejudices . . . Hence the other can recognize himself in him.

And if we have been recognized for one day, one hour, one instant, as a human being by a human being, let us love that being as ourselves—he is our soul.

And if we have encountered one day, one hour, one instant, a human being stripped naked, let us love that being as ourselves, for he is our soul.